The Ultimate Lasagna Cookbook!

80 Best and Most Delicious Lasagna Recipes

BY

Stephanie Sharp

Copyright © 2019 by Stephanie Sharp

License Notes

Copyright 2019 by Stephanie Sharp All rights reserved.

No part of this Book may be transmitted or reproduced into any format for any means without the proper permission of the Author. This includes electronic or mechanical methods, photocopying or printing.

The Reader assumes all risk when following any of the guidelines or ideas written as they are purely suggestion and for informational purposes. The Author has taken every precaution to ensure accuracy of the work but bears no responsibility if damages occur due to a misinterpretation of suggestions.

My deepest thanks for buying my book! Now that you have made this investment in time and money, you are now eligible for free e-books on a weekly basis! Once you subscribe by filling in the box below with your email address, you will start to receive free and discounted book offers for unique and informative books. There is nothing more to do! A reminder email will be sent to you a few days before the promotion expires so you will never have to worry about missing out on this amazing deal. Enter your email address below to get started. Thanks again for your purchase!

Just visit the link or scan QR-code to get started!

https://stephanie-sharp.subscribemenow.com

Table of Contents

Introduction 13

Lasagna Recipes with Pork 15

   Rich Pork Lasagna 16

   Rosemary Pork Lasagna 19

   Classic Pork Lasagna 22

   The Perfect Pork Lasagna 25

   Great Ground Pork Lasagna 28

   Colombian Lasagna 31

   Pork and Spinach Lasagna 35

   Pork Sausage Lasagna 38

   Pork and Kale Lasagna 41

Pork and Squash Lasagna 44

Lasagna Recipes with Beef 47

Simple Beef Lasagna 48

Sausage and Beef Lasagna 51

Pesto Beef Lasagna 54

Special Beef Lasagna 57

Beef and Zucchini Lasagna 60

Different Zucchini and Beef Lasagna 63

Great Beef and Veggies Lasagna 66

Mixed Veggies, Sausage and Beef Lasagna 69

Beef and Cabbage Lasagna 72

Beef and Mushroom Lasagna 75

Lasagna Recipes with Lamb 77

Lamb and Cheese Lasagna.. 78

Easy Lamb Lasagna 81

Crazy Lamb Lasagna.. 84

Elegant Lamb Lasagna... 87

Lamb and Spinach Lasagna... 90

Lamb and Eggplant Lasagna... 93

Lamb and Peas Lasagna 96

Lamb and Harissa Lasagna 99

Italian Lamb Lasagna 102

Fast Lamb Lasagna.. 105

Lasagna Recipes with Poultry.. 108

Simple Chicken and Cheese Lasagna........................ 109

Easy Chicken Lasagna 112

Light Chicken Lasagna.. 115

Delicious Chicken Lasagna... 118

Turkey Lasagna.. 120

Turkey and Zucchinis Lasagna 123

Turkey and Sweet Potato Lasagna 126

Duck Lasagna... 129

Duck and Wine Lasagna 132

Duck and Mushroom Lasagna.................................... 135

Lasagna Recipes with Fish and Seafood....................... 138

Simple Fish Lasagna 139

Seafood Lasagna 142

Fish and Zucchini Lasagna... 145

Fish and Green Pea Lasagna 148

Mixed Seafood Lasagna 151

Seafood and Mushrooms Lasagna 154

Salmon Lasagna 157

Salmon and Spinach Lasagna 160

Healthy Fish Lasagna 163

Crab and Shrimp Lasagna 166

Shrimp Lasagna 169

Shrimp and Broccoli Lasagna 172

Shrimp and Tomato Lasagna 175

Great Italian Shrimp Lasagna 178

Shrimp and Lobster Lasagna 181

Vegan Lasagna Recipes 184

    Tofu Lasagna 185

    Colored Veggie Lasagna 188

    Vegan Lasagna 192

    Fast Vegan Lasagna 195

    Special Veggie Lasagna 198

    Zucchini Lasagna 201

    Carrot Lasagna 204

    Lentils Lasagna 207

    Broccoli and Carrot Lasagna 210

    Celery Lasagna 213

    Squash Lasagna 217

    Squash and Spinach Lasagna 220

Squash and Caramelized Onion Lasagna 223

Leek Lasagna.. 226

Swiss Chard Lasagna 229

Dessert Lasagna Recipes.. 233

Peanut Butter Lasagna.. 234

Rich Chocolate Lasagna... 236

Strawberry Lasagna.. 239

Milky Lasagna... 242

Sweet Lasagna... 244

Minty Sweet Lasagna 247

Pumpkin Lasagna 249

Apple Lasagna... 252

Delicious Mango Lasagna 255

Ice Cream Lasagna 258

Conclusion 260

About the Author 261

Author's Afterthoughts 262

Introduction

We simply love lasagnas! I mean, what's not to love about them?

How can you not adore the delicious layers of veggies, white sauce, cheese and meat between sheets of pasta?

A lasagna is probably one of the easiest meals you can make at home! It is also really fun to make.

If you are hosting a family meal or a fancy dinner party, then you should really consider making an incredible lasagna.

You literally can't mess this up. You don't have to be an expert cook and you don't require special skills in the kitchen,

you just have to follow the directions and that's all!

All you need in order to make the best lasagna is to purchase the best ingredients and a great cooking guide.

Getting the ingredients is a simple task but a good lasagna recipes collection is sometimes hard to find.

That's why we are here today! We searched and gathered together the best lasagna recipes, compiling them into this simple and fascinating collection.

We can assure you that all the recipes are easy to make at home and that the outcome will always be perfect.

So, not only will we give you directions on how to start preparing and cooking the best savory lasagnas, such as pork, beef, lamb, poultry, fish and seafood. We will also show you how to make some incredible dessert lasagnas as well.

So, let's get started. Let's enjoy the best culinary experience and create some of the best lasagnas ever!

Lasagna Recipes with Pork

You have so many amazing options when it comes to making a delicious lasagna! Here are the best lasagna recipes made with pork!

Rich Pork Lasagna

Just taste this and be amazed!

Preparation Time: 10 minutes

Cooking Time: 1 hour and 40 minutes

Servings: 4

Ingredients:

- 1 yellow onion, chopped
- 2 tablespoons olive oil
- 5 garlic cloves, minced
- 1 carrot, chopped
- 1 and ½ pounds pork meat, ground
- A pinch of salt and black pepper
- ¼ cup tomato paste
- 30 ounces canned tomatoes, chopped
- 12 ounces no-boil lasagna noodles
- 2 teaspoons oregano, dried
- 1 pound mozzarella balls, sliced
- 2 cups ricotta cheese

Method:

1. Heat up a pot with the oil over medium high heat, add the garlic, carrots, onion, salt and pepper, toss and sauté for 6 minutes.

2. Add the meat, toss and brown for 5 minutes more.

3. Add the tomato paste, tomatoes, oregano, more salt and pepper, stir, cook for 10 minutes more and take off the heat.

4. Spread 1 cup of this mix on the bottom of a baking dish and then all 3 lasagna noodles over it.

5. Spread 1 more cup of pork mix over these noodles, then add half of the ricotta and the mozzarella.

6. Arrange 3 more lasagna noodles, then spread some more sauce, top with the rest of the noodles and then spread the rest of the sauce.

7. Layer the rest of the ricotta and then the rest of the mozzarella, cover the dish with tin foil and bake at 375 degrees F for 45 minutes.

8. Uncover the baking dish, cook for 30 minutes more, cool down a bit, slice the lasagna and serve it. Enjoy!

Rosemary Pork Lasagna

This is very tasty!

Preparation Time: 10 minutes

Cooking Time: 1 hour and 10 minutes

Servings: 4

Ingredients:

- 1 teaspoon olive oil
- 1 yellow onion, chopped
- 1 pound pork meat, ground
- 2 celery sticks, chopped
- 1 teaspoon rosemary, dried
- 2 ounces white wine
- 5 ounces chicken stock
- 2 tablespoons tomato paste
- 14 ounces canned tomatoes, chopped
- A pinch of salt and black pepper
- 1 teaspoon corn flour
- 3 ounces skimmed milk
- A pinch of nutmeg, dried
- 12 ounces lasagna sheets, dried
- 4 tablespoons parmesan, grated

Method:

1. Heat up a pan with the oil over medium heat, add the pork and brown it for a few minutes.

2. Add the wine, onion, celery and the rosemary, bring to a boil and cook for 10 minutes.

3. Add the stock, tomato paste, tomatoes, salt and pepper, stir and boil for 30 minutes more.

4. Add the corn flour, stir and take off the heat.

5. In a bowl, mix the milk with nutmeg and whisk.

6. Spoon a third of the meat on the bottom of a greased baking dish, then arrange 2 lasagna sheets over it.

7. Spread a third of the milk, then sprinkle some of the parmesan and top with 2 more lasagna sheets.

8. Repeat with the rest of the meat, milk and lasagna sheets and top with the rest of the parmesan.

9. Bake at 390 degrees F for 30 minutes, cool down a bit, slice and serve.

Enjoy!

Classic Pork Lasagna

Here's a classic lasagna you have to try!

Preparation Time: 10 minutes

Cooking Time: 1 hour and 10 minutes

Servings: 4

Ingredients:

- 1 pound pork meat, ground
- 16 ounces lasagna noodles, cooked
- 1/8 teaspoon sugar
- A pinch of salt and pepper
- 1 and ½ teaspoons basil, dried
- 9 ounces tomato sauce
- 1 pound cottage cheese
- 28 ounces canned tomatoes, crushed
- 3 eggs
- ¾ cup parmesan, grated
- 1 tablespoon parsley, chopped
- 1 garlic clove, minced
- ½ teaspoon oregano, dried
- ½ cup yellow onion, chopped
- 1 pound mozzarella, shredded

Method:

1. Heat up a pan over medium heat, add the meat and brown it for 3-4 minutes.

2. Add the tomato sauce, tomatoes, garlic, parsley, onion, oregano, sugar, basil, salt and pepper, toss and simmer everything for 30 minutes.

3. In a bowl, mix the eggs with salt, pepper, cottage cheese and parmesan and stir.

4. Arrange 2 layers of lasagna noodles on the bottom of a baking dish, then add ½ of the cheese mix, then half of the mozzarella and top with half of the meat.

5. Repeat with the rest of the lasagna, cheese, mix and meat and sprinkle the remaining mozzarella at the end.

6. Bake the lasagna at 375 degrees F for 35 minutes, cool down a bit, slice and serve.

Enjoy!

The Perfect Pork Lasagna

This is really a delicious lasagna!

Preparation Time: 10 minutes

Cooking Time: 1 hour

Servings: 4

Ingredients:

- 5 ounces cream cheese
- 6 ounces lasagna sheets, dried
- A handful basil, chopped
- 20 ounces canned tomatoes, chopped
- A pinch of salt and black pepper
- 1 pound pork meat, ground
- 2 garlic cloves, minced
- 1 tablespoon olive oil
- 3 ounces cheddar cheese, grated
- 1 egg, whisked

Method:

1. Heat up a pan with the oil over medium heat, add the pork, toss and brown for 3-4 minutes.

2. Add the garlic and the onion, toss and cook for 10 minutes more.

3. Add the tomatoes, basil, salt and pepper, toss and cook for 15 minutes.

4. In a bowl, mix the cream cheese with the cheddar and the egg and whisk well.

5. Spoon a layer of the sauce in a greased baking sheet, then arrange lasagna sheets on top.

6. Continue with some of the cream cheese and then repeat with the rest of the lasagna sheets, pork mix and top with a layer of cream cheese mix.

7. Bake the lasagna at 370 degrees F for 30 minutes, cool down a bit, slice and serve.

Enjoy!

Great Ground Pork Lasagna

This is the best ground pork lasagna!

Preparation Time: 10 minutes

Cooking Time: 1 hour and 10 minutes

Servings: 6

Ingredients:

- 3 tablespoons butter
- 1 yellow onion, chopped
- 1 pound pork meat, ground
- 2 garlic cloves, minced
- 1 teaspoon oregano, dried
- 1 tablespoon basil, chopped
- ¼ cup chili sauce
- 1 pound lasagna sheets, cooked
- A pinch of salt and black pepper
- 1 cup béchamel sauce
- 1 cup tomato sauce
- 6 mozzarella slices
- For the béchamel sauce:
- 2 teaspoons onion, chopped
- 1 tablespoon butter
- 1 and ½ cups milk
- A pinch of salt and white pepper
- 2 tablespoons flour
- A pinch of nutmeg, ground

Method:

1. Heat up a pan over medium heat, add 1 tablespoon butter, melt it, add 2 teaspoons onion, nutmeg, salt, pepper and flour, whisk well and cook for 2-3 minutes.

2. Add the milk, whisk, simmer for 20 minutes, strain and leave aside for now.

3. Heat up a pan with 3 tablespoons butter over medium heat, add 1 onion, toss and cook for 3-4 minutes.

4. Add the meat, garlic, basil and oregano, toss and cook for 5 minutes.

5. Add the chili sauce, salt and pepper, cover the pan, cook everything for 5 minutes more and take off the heat.

6. Layer lasagna sheets in a baking dish, add some of the béchamel sauce and then some of the meat mixture.

7. Repeat with the rest of the ingredients, top with mozzarella slices, bake at 300 degrees F for 35 minutes, cool down a bit, slice and serve.

Enjoy!

Colombian Lasagna

You won't regret trying this recipe today!

Preparation Time: 10 minutes

Cooking Time: 2 hours

Servings: 4

Ingredients:

- 1 pound lasagna noodles, cooked
- 4 chicken breasts, bone-in, skinless
- 1 pound pork loin
- 1 cup tomato sauce
- 2 tablespoons olive oil
- 3 tablespoons butter
- 2 cups carrots, grated
- 1 yellow onion, chopped
- 1 red bell pepper, chopped
- 3 cups chicken stock
- 5 garlic cloves, minced
- ½ teaspoon cumin, ground
- ½ cup ketchup
- 3 cups milk
- Salt and black pepper to the taste
- ¼ cup flour
- 1 cup parmesan, grated
- 2 pound mozzarella, shredded

Method:

1. Put the pork and the chicken in a pot, add water to cover, bring to a boil over medium heat, cook for 12 minutes and remove the chicken from the pot.

2. Cook the pork for 10 minutes more and also remove from the pot.

3. Cool the meat down and shred it all.

4. Heat up a pan with the butter and the oil over medium heat, add the carrot, onions and bell pepper, stir and cook for 7 minutes.

5. Add the tomato paste, cumin, ketchup, salt, pepper and the garlic, stir and cook for 3 minutes more.

6. Add the stock and the shredded meat, toss and cook for 25 minutes.

7. Put the milk in a pan, heat it up over medium heat, add the flour and the nutmeg, whisk well for 2 minutes and take off the heat.

8. Grease a baking dish with some oil and layer some of the lasagna noodles.

9. Add some of the milk mix, spread some of the meat mixture and then top with some of the mozzarella.

10. Repeat the action with the rest of the ingredients, sprinkle the parmesan on top, bake at 375 degrees F for 40 minutes, cool down, slice and serve.

Enjoy!

Pork and Spinach Lasagna

It's tasty and rich! You have to try it soon!

Preparation Time: 10 minutes

Cooking Time: 40 minutes

Servings: 6

Ingredients:

- 1 tablespoon olive oil
- 1 pound pork meat, ground
- 2 garlic cloves, minced
- 5 ounces mushrooms, sliced
- 7 ounces crème fraîche
- 4 ounces spinach, chopped
- 12 ounces lasagna sheets, cooked
- 2 ounces cheddar cheese, shredded
- A pinch of salt and black pepper
- For the thyme sauce;
- 2 tablespoons tomato paste
- 1 pound tomatoes, chopped
- 1 teaspoon sugar
- 1 tablespoon thyme, chopped

Method:

1. Heat up a pan with the oil over medium heat, add the pork and brown it for 3-4 minutes.

2. Add the mushrooms, garlic, crème fraîche, salt, pepper and spinach, toss, bring to a simmer and cook for 5 minutes more.

3. In a bowl, mix the tomato paste with tomatoes, sugar and thyme and whisk well.

4. Spread some of the sauce into a greased baking dish, then layer some of the lasagna sheets, then continue with some of the pork mix.

5. Continue with the rest of the ingredients, sprinkle the cheese on top, cook at 375 degrees F for 30 minutes, cool down a bit, slice and serve.

Enjoy!

Pork Sausage Lasagna

This is really awesome!

Preparation Time: 10 minutes

Cooking Time: 1 hour and 10 minutes

Servings: 8

Ingredients:

- 1 yellow onion, chopped
- 1 garlic clove, minced
- 1 pound pork sausage, casings removed and chopped
- 1 tablespoon basil, chopped
- 4 tablespoons parsley, chopped
- 1 teaspoon sugar
- 2 cups tomatoes, chopped
- 15 ounces tomato sauce
- 12 ounces lasagna noodles, cooked
- 12 ounces ricotta cheese
- ¼ cup parmesan, grated
- 1 tablespoon oregano, chopped
- 2 cups mozzarella cheese, shredded

Method:

1. Heat up a pan over medium heat, add the sausage, garlic and onion, toss and brown for 3-4 minutes.

2. Add half of the parsley, all the basil, tomato sauce, tomatoes and the sugar, stir, bring to a boil and simmer for 40 minutes.

3. In a bowl, mix the ricotta with half of the parmesan, the rest of the parsley and the oregano and stir well.

4. Spread 1 cup of the sausage mix on the bottom of a greased baking dish, then layer 4 lasagna noodles and top with 1 cup of the cheese mixture.

5. Continue the layers with the rest of the ingredients, sprinkle the rest of the parmesan and the mozzarella on top, bake covered at 350 degrees F for 30 minutes and uncovered for 15 minutes more.

6. Cool the lasagna down, slice and serve.

Enjoy!

Pork and Kale Lasagna

This is one of our favorite combinations!

Preparation Time: 10 minutes

Cooking Time: 1 hour and 15 minutes

Servings: 6

Ingredients:

- 2 tablespoons olive oil
- 3 pounds sweet sausage, casings removed and chopped
- 1 cup kale, chopped
- 6 cups tomato sauce
- 2 eggs, whisked
- 16 ounces ricotta cheese
- 1 pound mozzarella, shredded
- 2 cups parmesan, grated
- 12 ounces lasagna noodles, cooked

Method:

1. Heat up a pan with the oil over medium high heat, add the sausage, toss and brown for 10 minutes.

2. Add the tomato sauce, toss, cook for a couple more minutes and take off the heat.

3. In a bowl, mix the eggs with the kale, ricotta and almost all the parmesan and stir well.

4. Spread a third of the sausage mix on the bottom of a baking dish, then add a third of the lasagna noodles and continue with a third of the kale mix.

5. Repeat with the rest of the ingredients, sprinkle the rest of the parmesan at the end, bake covered with tin foil at 400 degrees F for 40 minutes and uncovered for 20 minutes more.

6. Cool the lasagna down, slice and serve.

Enjoy!

Pork and Squash Lasagna

This looks incredible!

Preparation Time: 10 minutes

Cooking Time: 2 hours

Servings: 10

Ingredients:

- 1 pound pork meat, ground
- 1 butternut squash, halved and deseeded
- ½ cup water
- 2 cups ricotta cheese
- 1/3 cup light cream
- 2 teaspoons olive oil
- 1 yellow onion, chopped
- 1 pound pork meat, ground
- 2 eggs, whisked
- 1 cup parmesan, grated
- 2 tablespoons oregano, chopped
- ¼ cup sage, chopped
- 1 tablespoon thyme, chopped
- A pinch of salt and black pepper
- 16 ounces lasagna noodles, cooked
- 1 pound mozzarella, shredded

Method:

1. Place squash halves on a lined baking sheet, add the water, bake at 375 degrees F or 50 minutes, cool the squash down, scoop flesh into a blender, pulse well, transfer to a bowl and mix with the light cream and the ricotta.

2. Heat up a pan with the oil over medium heat, add the onion, stir and cook for 6 minutes.

3. Add the pork, stir, brown for a few minutes more and take off the heat, add sage, oregano, eggs, parmesan, thyme, salt and pepper and stir well.

4. Spread a layer of the butternut squash mix on the bottom of a baking dish, then arrange a layer of the lasagna noodles.

5. Layer a third of the mozzarella, then continue with a layer of pork and lasagna noodles.

6. Add the rest of the pork mix, continue with the mozzarella, squash and top with the lasagna noodles.

7. Spread the rest of the mozzarella on top, cover the dish with tin foil, bake the lasagna for 30 minutes at 375 degrees F, then uncover and bake for 15 minutes more.

8. Cool the lasagna, slice and serve. Enjoy!

Lasagna Recipes with Beef

These next recipes are really impressive. They are all so rich, textured and delicious and you have to try all of them as soon as possible!

Simple Beef Lasagna

It's always great to try a good lasagna! Now, try this one!

Preparation Time: 10 minutes

Cooking Time: 1 hour

Servings: 4

Ingredients:

- 10 ounces whole wheat lasagna noodles, cooked
- 15 ounces cottage cheese
- 1 pound beef, ground
- 2 eggs, whisked
- 2 garlic cloves, minced
- ½ cup parmesan, grated
- ½ teaspoon garlic powder
- 1 teaspoon oregano, dried
- 2 cups mozzarella, shredded
- 25 ounces jarred tomato-basil pasta sauce
- A pinch of salt and black pepper

Method:

1. Heat up a pan over medium heat, add the beef, garlic, garlic powder, salt, pepper and the oregano, stir and brown for 10 minutes.

2. In a bowl, mix the eggs with the cottage and the parmesan and stir well.

3. Put 4 lasagna noodles on the bottom on a greased baking dish, then add a layer of the tomato and basil sauce, then spread a layer of the beef mix and continue with the cottage cheese mix.

4. Repeat the layers, sprinkle the mozzarella on top, cover the dish with tin foil and bake the lasagna for 30 minutes at 350 degrees F.

5. Uncover the dish, bake for 10 minutes more, cool the lasagna down, slice and serve.

Enjoy!

Sausage and Beef Lasagna

Have you ever tried such an intense combination?

Preparation Time: 10 minutes

Cooking Time: 2 hours and 30 minutes

Servings: 6

Ingredients:

- 1 pound Italian sausage, casings removed
- 1 pound beef meat, ground
- 1 teaspoon Italian seasoning
- A pinch of salt and black pepper
- ½ cup yellow onion, chopped
- 4 tablespoons parsley, chopped
- 2 garlic cloves, minced
- 12 ounces lasagna noodles, cooked
- 1 egg
- 13 ounces canned tomato sauce
- 12 ounces tomato paste
- 27 ounces canned tomatoes, crushed
- ½ cup water
- 2 tablespoons sugar
- 1 and ½ tablespoons basil, chopped
- 1 pound mozzarella, sliced
- ¾ cup parmesan, grated
- ½ teaspoon fennel seeds

Method:

1. Heat up a pot over medium heat, add the beef, sausage, onion and garlic, stir and brown for 5-6 minutes.

2. Add tomato paste, tomato sauce, water, tomatoes, salt, pepper, basil, Italian seasoning, sugar, fennel and half of the parsley, stir, bring to a simmer and cook for 1 hour and 30 minutes.

3. In a bowl, mix the ricotta with the egg, salt, pepper and the rest of the parsley and stir.

4. Spread 1 and ½ cups of meat mixture on the bottom of a baking dish, arrange 6 lasagna noodles over it, then spread half of the ricotta mix and top with a third of the mozzarella.

5. Continue with 1 and ½ cups meat mixture and sprinkle half of the parmesan.

6. Continue with the layers until you finish all the ingredients and top with the remaining parmesan and mozzarella.

7. Cover the dish with tin foil, bake at 375 degrees F for 25 minutes, then uncover the dish and cook the lasagna for another 25 minutes.

8. Cool the lasagna down, slice and serve. Enjoy!

Pesto Beef Lasagna

You just have to try this today!

Preparation Time: 10 minutes

Cooking Time: 1 hour

Servings: 8

Ingredients:

- 16 ounces lasagna noodles, cooked
- 25 ounces cottage cheese
- 14 ounces ricotta cheese
- 2 eggs, whisked
- 12 cup basil pesto
- A pinch of salt and black pepper
- 2 and ½ cups mozzarella cheese, shredded
- 1 pound beef meat, ground
- ½ cup yellow onion, chopped
- 45 ounces tomato and basil pasta sauce
- Cooking spray

Method:

1. In a bowl, mix the ricotta cheese with the cottage cheese, pesto, salt, pepper, 1 cup mozzarella and the eggs and stir.

2. Heat up a pan over medium heat, add the onion and the beef, stir and brown for 7 minutes.

3. Add the pasta sauce, stir and take off the heat.

4. Grease a baking dish with the cooking spray, spread 1 cup of beef mix and top with 3 lasagna noodles.

5. Add 2 and ½ cups cheese mix, then continue with 3 lasagna noodles, 2 cups beef mix and 3 more lasagna noodles.

6. Sprinkle the rest of the mozzarella on top, cover the dish with tin foil, bake at 375 degrees F for 40 minutes, then uncover and bake for 20 minutes more.

7. Cool the lasagna a bit, slice and serve.

Enjoy!

Special Beef Lasagna

It's a tasty and so special recipe!

Preparation Time: 10 minutes

Cooking Time: 1 hour

Servings: 10

Ingredients:

- 2 teaspoons basil, dried
- 2 pound beef, ground
- 2 teaspoons oregano, dried
- A pinch of salt and black pepper
- ½ teaspoon red pepper flakes, crushed
- 6 cups marinara sauce
- ¼ cup parsley, chopped
- 16 ounces lasagna noodles, cooked
- 15 ounces ricotta cheese
- ½ pound provolone cheese, sliced
- 1 egg
- ½ pound mozzarella, sliced
- 1 cup parmesan, grated

Method:

1. Heat up a pot over medium heat, add the beef and brown for 3-4 minutes.

2. Add basil, oregano, salt, pepper, pepper flakes and the marinara sauce, stir, cook for 8 minutes more and take off the heat.

3. In a bowl, mix the ricotta with salt, pepper, parsley and the egg and stir well.

4. Spread 1 and ½ cups meat sauce on the bottom of a baking dish, layer 5 lasagna noodles, then, add 1/3 provolone cheese, then 1 and ½ cups meat sauce, ¼ parmesan, ¼ mozzarella and 1/3 ricotta mix.

5. Continue until you finish all the ingredients, top with a layer of parmesan and mozzarella, cover the dish with tin foil, bake at 375 for 40 minutes, cool down, slice and serve.

Enjoy!

Beef and Zucchini Lasagna

Get ready for a real treat!

Preparation Time: 10 minutes

Cooking Time: 1 hour and 40 minutes

Servings: 8

Ingredients:

- 1 pound beef meat, ground
- 12 ounces tomato paste
- 1 yellow onion, chopped
- 2 eggs, whisked
- 2 cups ricotta cheese
- 2 tablespoons basil, chopped
- 4 garlic cloves, minced
- 1 tablespoon parsley, chopped
- 1 cup parmesan, grated
- 2 tablespoons oregano, chopped
- A pinch of salt and black pepper
- 3 zucchinis, cut into long strips similar to lasagna noodles
- 2 tablespoons brown sugar
- 2 cups mozzarella, sliced
- 14 ounces canned tomatoes, chopped

Method:

1. Heat up a pot over medium heat, add the beef, garlic and onion, stir and cook for 10 minutes.

2. Add salt, pepper, sugar, basil, oregano, pepper flakes, tomato paste and tomatoes, stir and simmer for 30 minutes.

3. In a bowl, mix half of the parmesan with the ricotta, salt, pepper and the parsley and stir.

4. Arrange 1/3 of the zucchini lasagna sheets on the bottom of a baking dish, spread half of the ricotta mix, then half of the mozzarella and 1/3 of the meat.

5. Repeat with the remaining layers of zucchini, ricotta, meat sauce and mozzarella.

6. Sprinkle the parmesan on top, introduce the lasagna in the oven, bake at 375 degrees F for 1 hour, cool down, slice and serve.

Enjoy!

Different Zucchini and Beef Lasagna

Try this unique lasagna recipe!

Preparation Time: 10 minutes

Cooking Time: 1 hour and 10 minutes

Servings: 6

Ingredients:

- 1 pound beef meat, ground
- 1 green bell pepper, chopped
- 1 yellow onion, chopped
- 15 ounces tomato and basil pasta sauce
- 2 cups ricotta cheese
- 1 egg, whisked
- 2 big zucchinis, thinly sliced lengthwise
- 15 ounces lasagna noodles, cooked
- ½ cup parmesan, grated
- 1 cup mozzarella, shredded

Method:

1. Heat up a pot over medium heat, add the beef, green bell pepper and the onion, stir and brown for 5 minutes.

2. Add the pasta sauce, stir and simmer for 20 minutes more.

3. In a bowl, mix the ricotta with the egg and whisk.

4. Spread ¼ of the meat sauce on the bottom of a baking dish, layer 3 lasagna noodles, then 1/3 of the zucchini slices.

5. Continue with 1/3 ricotta mix, then add ¼ meat sauce.

6. Continue with the remaining layers, cover the dish with tin foil and bake at 375 degrees F for 40 minutes.

7. Sprinkle the parmesan and the mozzarella all over, bake uncovered for 10 minutes more, cool down, slice and serve.

Enjoy!

Great Beef and Veggies Lasagna

This is so textured! You are going to love it!

Preparation Time: 10 minutes

Cooking Time: 1 hour and 10 minutes

Servings: 6

Ingredients:

- 1 pound beef meat, ground
- 1 tablespoon olive oil
- 1 zucchini, chopped
- 1 carrots, finely grated
- 1 red bell pepper, chopped
- 15 ounces canned tomato, onion and roasted garlic pasta sauce
- ¼ cup basil, chopped
- 8 ounces lasagna noodles, cooked
- 14 ounces canned béchamel sauce
- 1 cup pizza cheese, shredded

Method:

1. Heat up a pot with the oil over medium heat, add the meat, stir and brown for 5 minutes.

2. Add zucchini, bell pepper and carrot, stir and cook for 5 minutes.

3. Add pasta sauce, stir and simmer over medium heat for 6 minutes more.

4. Add the basil, stir and take off the heat.

5. Spoon 1/3 of this meat sauce on the bottom of the baking dish, then, layer 1/3 of the lasagna noodles, continue with 1/3 of the béchamel sauce.

6. Continue with the remaining ingredients, sprinkle the pizza cheese at the end, bake at 375 degrees F for 40 minutes, cool down a bit, slice and serve.

Enjoy!

Mixed Veggies, Sausage and Beef Lasagna

You simply have to try this special and amazing lasagna!

Preparation Time: 10 minutes

Cooking Time: 2 hours and 10 minutes

Servings: 8

Ingredients:

- 1 pound beef meat, ground
- ½ pound veal sausages, casings removed
- 2 garlic cloves, minced
- 2 yellow onions, chopped
- ½ teaspoon cumin seeds
- 1 teaspoon herbes de Provence
- A pinch of salt and black pepper
- 15 ounces tomato paste
- 14 ounces canned tomatoes, crushed
- ½ cup red wine
- 1 pound mixed veggies (bell peppers, zucchinis and mushrooms), grilled
- 1 cup ricotta cheese
- ¼ cup milk
- 1 egg, whisked
- 9 ounces lasagna noodles, cooked
- 2/3 cup parmesan, grated
- Cooking spray

Method:

1. Heat up a pot over medium heat, add the beef, the sausage, garlic and onions, stir and cook for 10 minutes

2. Add salt, pepper, herbs, cumin, tomato paste, wine and crushed tomatoes, stir, bring to a simmer and cook for 1 hour.

3. In a bowl, mix the ricotta with the milk and the egg and whisk.

4. Spread a layer of lasagna noodles on the bottom of a baking dish greased with cooking spray, add ½ of the meat sauce, then ½ of the grilled veggies and 1/3 of the ricotta.

5. Continue layering until you finish all the ingredients, sprinkle the parmesan on top, cover with tin foil, bake at 375 degrees F for 30 minutes, uncover the dish, bake the lasagna for 30 minutes more, cool down, slice and serve.

Enjoy!

Beef and Cabbage Lasagna

This is so awesome!

Preparation Time: 10 minutes

Cooking Time: 40 minutes

Servings: 16

Ingredients:

- 3 pounds ricotta cheese
- 1 cabbage head, leaves separated and blanched for 4-5 minutes
- ¼ cup parsley, chopped
- 1 and ½ cups parmesan, grated
- 3 eggs, whisked
- 2 pounds beef, browned
- 40 ounces marinara sauce
- 32 ounces mozzarella, shredded

Method:

1. In a bowl, mix the ricotta with parmesan, parsley and the eggs and whisk.

2. In another bowl, mix the beef with the marinara sauce and stir.

3. Spoon ¾ cup of meat sauce on the bottom of a baking dish, add a layer of cabbage leaves, the spread half of the ricotta cheese, then add some more meat sauce and so on until you finish all the ingredients.

4. Top with the mozzarella, bake the lasagna at 350 degrees F for 30 minutes, cool down, slice and serve.

Enjoy!

Beef and Mushroom Lasagna

The combination is right! Trust us!

Preparation Time: 10 minutes

Cooking Time: 1 hour

Servings: 6

Ingredients:

- 14 ounces cream of mushroom soup
- ¼ cup milk
- 2 cups mushroom pasta sauce
- 1 pound beef, ground
- 14 ounces lasagna noodles, cooked
- 1 cup mozzarella cheese, shredded

Method:

1. In a bowl, mix the cream of mushroom soup with the milk and whisk well.

2. In a separate bowl, mix the beef with the mushroom pasta sauce and stir.

3. Layer half of the beef mix in a baking dish, then add 3 lasagna noodles and 1 cup mushroom soup.

4. Continue with 3 noodles, the rest of the beef, the rest of the noodles and the remaining mushroom soup.

5. Sprinkle the cheese on top, cover the dish with tin foil, bake at 360 degrees F for 30 minutes, cool down, slice and serve. Enjoy!

Lasagna Recipes with Lamb

We bet you didn't know that you could make so many amazing lasagnas. It's time for you to discover the best and most delicious lasagna recipes made with lamb.

Lamb and Cheese Lasagna

This is a delicious Greek lasagna!

Preparation Time: 10 minutes

Cooking Time: 1 hour and 10 minutes

Servings: 8

Ingredients:

- 1 and ½ cups yellow onion, chopped
- 2 teaspoons olive oil
- 1 tablespoon rosemary, chopped
- 1 and ½ tablespoons garlic, minced
- 18 ounces lamb meat, ground
- 1 and ¼ cups chicken stock
- A pinch of salt and black pepper
- 28 ounces canned tomatoes, crushed
- 15 ounces canned tomato sauce
- 1 and ¼ cups ricotta cheese
- 14 ounces lasagna noodles, cooked
- ½ teaspoon lemon rind, grated
- 3 ounces feta cheese, crumbled
- Cooking spray
- 3 tablespoons parsley, chopped

Method:

1. Heat up a pot with the oil over medium heat, add the onion, garlic, rosemary and the lamb, stir and brown for 10 minutes.

2. Add the stock, salt, pepper, tomatoes and tomato sauce, stir, simmer for 5-6 minutes and take off the heat.

3. In a bowl, mix the ricotta with the lemon rind and stir.

4. Spread 1 tablespoon of ricotta on one side of the lasagna noodles.

5. Spread 2 cups lamb sauce on the bottom of a baking dish greased with cooking spray, arrange 3 lasagna noodles with the ricotta side up and add 2 more cups of meat sauce.

6. Continue with the layers until you finish all the ingredients, sprinkle the feta cheese on top, cover the dish with tin foil, bake at 375 degrees F for 40 minutes, uncover, cool down, slice, divide between plates, sprinkle parsley on top and serve.

Enjoy!

Easy Lamb Lasagna

This is an easy dish everyone can make at home!

Preparation Time: 10 minutes

Cooking Time: 3 hours and 40 minutes

Servings: 4

Ingredients:

- 1 pound lamb fillets
- 1 tablespoon olive oil
- 1 garlic clove, minced
- 1 rosemary spring, chopped
- 15 ounces tomato passata
- 14 ounces canned béchamel sauce
- 3 tablespoons parmesan, grated
- 8 ounces lasagna sheets, boiled
- 2 tablespoons breadcrumbs
- 2 mozzarella balls, torn
- 1 tablespoons dressed chicory leaves, chopped

Method:

1. Heat up a pot with the oil over medium heat, add the lamb, rosemary and garlic, toss and cook for 6 minutes.

2. Add the passata, bring to a boil, cover the pot with tin foil and bake at 350 degrees F for 3 hours.

3. Cool the mixture down and shred the meat using 2 forks.

4. Spread a layer of the lamb mix on the bottom of a baking dish, add a layer of lasagna sheets, then spread a layer of béchamel and sprinkle some of the mozzarella.

5. Repeat the layers until you finish all the ingredients, top with mozzarella, parmesan and breadcrumbs, bake the lasagna at 375 degrees F for 40 minutes, cool it down, slice, divide between plates, sprinkle the chicory on top and serve.

Enjoy!

Crazy Lamb Lasagna

This is an original and special lamb lasagna!

Preparation Time: 10 minutes

Cooking Time: 7 hours

Servings: 6

Ingredients:

- 3 and ½ pounds lamb stew meat
- 40 ounces canned tomatoes, chopped
- 6 ounces tomato paste
- ¼ cup oregano, chopped
- 1 yellow onion, chopped
- 4 garlic cloves, minced
- A pinch of salt and black pepper
- 45 ounces ricotta cheese
- 2 pounds mozzarella cheese, grated
- ¼ cup basil, chopped+ 2 tablespoons for serving
- ¼ cup parsley, chopped
- 1 and ½ cups parmesan, grated
- 2 eggs, whisked
- A drizzle of olive oil
- 20 ounces lasagna noodles, cooked

Method:

1. In a slow cooker, combine the lamb meat with tomatoes, tomato paste, onion, oregano, garlic, salt and pepper, cover and cook on High for 6 hours.

2. Shred the meat using 2 forks and stir and leave aside.

3. In a bowl, mix the ricotta with the mozzarella, parsley, basil and the eggs and stir well.

4. Spoon a layer of lamb sauce in a baking dish greased with olive oil, add a layer of lasagna noodles, then add 1/3 of the parmesan and top with the ricotta mix.

5. Repeat with the rest of the ingredients, top with the rest of the parmesan, cover the dish, bake at 375 degrees F for 40 minutes, uncover and bake for 10 minutes more.

6. Slice, divide between plates, sprinkle the rest of the basil in top and serve.

Enjoy!

Elegant Lamb Lasagna

This is perfect for a fancy dinner party!

Preparation Time: 10 minutes

Cooking Time: 5 hours and 30 minutes

Servings: 5

Ingredients:

- 2 pounds lamb shoulder
- 4 garlic cloves, minced
- 3 rosemary springs, chopped
- 2 tablespoons olive oil+ drizzle
- A pinch of salt and black pepper
- 2 ounces smoked pancetta, chopped
- 3 ounces carrots, grated
- 3 ounces celery, chopped
- 3 ounces yellow onion, chopped
- 1 bottle red wine
- 1 tablespoon tomato puree
- 3 ounces passata
- 2 cups lamb stock
- 6 tomatoes, chopped
- 4 tablespoons parmesan, grated
- 2 tablespoons fontina cheese
- 2 teaspoons mustard
- 2 tablespoons butter, melted
- 2 cups milk, warm
- 16 ounces lasagna sheets, cooked

Method:

1. In a slow cooker, mix the lamb with garlic, rosemary, salt, pepper, pancetta and a drizzle of oil, cover, cook on High for 5 hours and shred the meat.

2. Heat up a pot with the oil over medium high heat, add carrots, celery and onion, stir and cook for 5 minutes.

3. Add tomatoes, stock, passata, tomato puree, wine and the lamb, stir, bring to a simmer and cook for 20 minutes.

4. In a bowl, mix the butter with the mustard, fontina cheese and milk and whisk well.

5. Spread a layer of the lamb mix in a baking dish, add a layer of lasagna sheets, then continue with a layer of cheese and milk mixture.

6. Repeat the layers, top with the parmesan, bake at 370 degrees F for 30 minutes, cool down, slice and serve.

Enjoy!

Lamb and Spinach Lasagna

Just gather all the ingredients and make this tonight!

Preparation Time: 10 minutes

Cooking Time: 2 hours

Servings: 10

Ingredients:

- 1 and ½ pounds lamb leg, boneless and ground
- 5 tablespoons olive oil
- 5 ounces butter, melted
- 4 tablespoons yellow onion, chopped
- 4 tablespoons carrot, chopped
- 4 garlic cloves, minced
- 5 ounces white wine
- 14 tablespoons milk, warm
- 1 teaspoon nutmeg, ground
- 2 pounds tomatoes, chopped
- 5 ounces canned béchamel sauce
- 8 tablespoons parmesan, grated
- 18 ounces lasagna sheets, cooked
- For the spinach layer:
- ½ pound spinach leaves
- 1 yellow onion, chopped
- 1 garlic clove, minced
- 1 pound ricotta cheese
- 1 egg, whisked

Directions:

1. Heat up a pot with the oil and the butter over medium heat, add the garlic, carrot and 4 tablespoons onion, stir and cook for 5 minutes.

2. Add the meat, stir and cook for 10 minutes.

3. Add the tomatoes, the wine, the nutmeg and the milk, stir, bring to a simmer and cook for 50 minutes.

4. In a bowl, mix 1 onion with spinach, garlic, egg and ricotta and whisk well.

5. Spoon some of the lamb sauce on the bottom of a baking dish, then layer some of the lasagna sheets, also add a layer of spinach mix, some of the béchamel and some of the parmesan.

6. Repeat the layers until you finish all the ingredients, sprinkle parmesan on top, introduce in the oven and bake at 370 degrees F for 1 hour.

7. Slice, divide between plates and serve.

Enjoy!

Lamb and Eggplant Lasagna

Here's a great Mediterranean dish!

Preparation Time: 10 minutes

Cooking Time: 1 hour and 30 minutes

Servings: 6

Ingredients:

- 1 and ½ pounds lamb meat, ground
- 1 yellow onion, chopped
- 1 celery stalk, chopped
- 2 thyme springs, chopped
- 1 tablespoon garlic, minced
- 3 tablespoons olive oil
- 16 ounces lasagna noodles, cooked
- 2 eggplants, chopped
- 2 bay leaves
- ½ cup red wine
- 28 ounces canned tomatoes, chopped
- A pinch of salt and black pepper
- For the béchamel sauce:
- 1 quart cream milk
- 4 cloves
- 1 brown onion, halved
- 2 bay leaves
- 3 ounces butter, soft
- 6 black peppercorns
- 1 cup pecorino cheese, grated
- 1 cup flour

Method:

1. Heat up a pot with the olive oil over medium high heat, add the yellow onion, celery, thyme and garlic, stir and cook for 5 minutes.

2. Add the lamb, stir and brown for 5 more minutes.

3. Add the eggplant, 2 bay leaves, wine, tomatoes, salt and pepper, stir, bring to a simmer and cook for 35 minutes.

4. Heat up another pot with the milk over medium heat, add the brown onion, cloves, 2 bay leaves, butter, peppercorns, flour and pecorino cheese, whisk, simmer for 10 minutes, take off the heat and strain into a bowl.

5. Spread a layer of the lamb and eggplant sauce on the bottom of a baking dish, add a layer of lasagna sheets and then a layer of béchamel sauce.

6. Repeat the layers until you finish all the ingredients, bake the lasagna at 375 degrees F for 40 minutes, cool down, slice and serve.

Enjoy!

Lamb and Peas Lasagna

This is really something worth trying today! Everyone will love it!

Preparation Time: 10 minutes

Cooking Time: 1 hour and 20 minutes

Servings: 6

Ingredients:

- 16 ounces tomato passata
- 1 yellow onion, chopped
- 1 tablespoon olive oil
- 1 pound lamb meat, ground
- ½ teaspoon chili flakes, crushed
- 2 garlic cloves, minced
- 1 teaspoon allspice, ground
- ¼ teaspoon cinnamon powder
- 2 tablespoons tomato paste
- 1 tablespoon rosemary, chopped
- 1/3 cup mint, chopped
- 15 ounces lasagna sheets, cooked
- 3 ounces baby rocket
- ¼ cup corn flour
- 2/3 cup peas
- 2 and ½ cups Greek yogurt
- 1 cup mozzarella, shredded
- 1 egg, whisked
- 2 teaspoons lemon zest, grated

Method:

1. Heat up a pot with the oil over medium heat, add the onion, garlic and chili flakes, stir and cook for 3 minutes.

2. Add the meat, stir and brown for 5 minutes.

3. Add allspice, cinnamon, rosemary, rocket, mint and tomato paste, stir and cook for 10 minutes more.

4. In a bowl, mix the yogurt with the egg, corn flour and lemon zest and whisk well.

5. Spread a layer of the tomato passata on the bottom of a baking dish, layer 3 lasagna noodles, then add a layer of the meat sauce, a layer of peas, 1/3 of the mozzarella and a layer for the yogurt mix.

6. Continue with the layers until you finish all the ingredients, sprinkle the mozzarella at the end, introduce the dish in the oven and bake at 370 degrees F for 40 minutes.

7. Slice, divide between plates and serve.

Enjoy!

Lamb and Harissa Lasagna

Here's an Algerian lasagna dish you should try!

Preparation Time: 10 minutes

Cooking Time: 2 hours

Servings: 6

Ingredients:

- 1 pound lamb meat, ground
- ½ cup olive oil
- 1 yellow onion, chopped
- A pinch of salt and black pepper
- 1 tablespoon harissa
- 2 teaspoons cayenne pepper
- 1 garlic clove, minced
- ¼ teaspoon caraway seeds
- ½ teaspoon cumin, ground
- 1 tablespoon tomato paste
- 7 ounces canned chickpeas, drained
- 2 cups tomato puree
- 1 cup water
- 3 potatoes, cubed
- 1 pound lasagna sheets, cooked
- 15 ounces ricotta cheese
- 2 eggs, whisked
- 2 cups gruyere cheese, grated
- 2 cups mozzarella, grated

Directions:

1. Heat up a pan with the oil over medium high heat, add the onions and the garlic, stir and cook for 10 minutes.

2. Add the meat, stir and cook for 7 minutes more.

3. Add harissa, cayenne, cumin, tomato paste, caraway, tomato puree, water and chickpeas, stir and cook for 10 minutes.

4. Add the potatoes, salt and pepper, stir and cook for 10 minutes.

5. In a bowl, mix the ricotta with the eggs, salt, pepper and half of the gruyere and stir.

6. Spread a layer of the lamb mix on the bottom of a baking dish, add a layer of lasagna sheets, then spread a layer of ricotta cheese and sprinkle some of the mozzarella.

7. Continue with the layers until the ingredients are done, sprinkle the rest of the gruyere on top, cover with tin foil, bake at 375 degrees F for 1 hour, cool down, slice and serve.

Enjoy!

Italian Lamb Lasagna

This is the real deal! It's so amazing!

Preparation Time: 10 minutes

Cooking Time: 1 hour and 15 minutes

Servings: 4

Ingredients:

- 5 ounces lasagna sheets, cooked
- 1 and ½ pounds lamb meat, ground
- 15 ounces tomato passata
- A handful cherry tomatoes, halved
- 2 celery stalks, chopped
- 2 carrots, grated
- 1 yellow onion, chopped
- 1 rosemary, spring, chopped
- ½ glass of red wine
- 3 tablespoons olive oil
- 1 cup lamb stock
- 3 tablespoons parmesan, grated
- 3 ounces béchamel sauce

Method:

1. Heat up a pan with the oil over medium high heat, add the onion, carrots, celery, rosemary and tomatoes, stir and cook for 6 minutes.

2. Add the meat, stir and brown for 4-5 minutes.

3. Add the stock, wine and the passata, stir, simmer for 15 minutes and take off the heat.

4. Spread a layer of the lamb sauce in a baking dish, then add a layer of lasagna sheets, continue with a layer of béchamel and top with some of the parmesan.

5. Repeat the layers until you finish all the ingredients, sprinkle the rest of the parmesan on top, bake for 50 minutes at 360 degrees F, cool down, slice and serve.

Enjoy!

Fast Lamb Lasagna

Make a tasty lamb lasagna in your slow cooker today!

Preparation Time: 10 minutes

Cooking Time: 1 hour and 10 minutes

Servings: 4

Ingredients:

- 1 and ½ pounds lamb meat, ground
- 2 tablespoons olive oil
- 2 carrots, chopped
- 2 yellow onions, chopped
- 1 garlic clove, minced
- 2 bay leaves
- 2 tablespoons tomato puree
- 2 tablespoons parsley, chopped
- 2 tablespoons basil, chopped
- 14 ounces white wine
- 14 ounces veal stock
- 15 ounces canned tomatoes, chopped
- 1 pound lasagna sheets, cooked
- 10 ounces béchamel sauce
- 2 mozzarella balls, shredded
- 4 ounces parmesan, grated
- A pinch of salt and black pepper

Method:

1. Heat up a pot with the oil over medium heat, add the onions, garlic, bay leaves and carrots, stir and cook for 5 minutes.

2. Add the lamb, stir and cook for 7 minutes more.

3. Add tomato puree, parsley, basil, wine, stock, salt, pepper and tomatoes, whisk, bring to a simmer and cook for 20 minutes.

4. Spread a layer of the meat sauce on the bottom of a baking dish, then arrange a layer of lasagna sheets.

5. Continue with some of the parmesan and some of the mozzarella.

6. Continue with the rest of the ingredients, sprinkle the remaining mozzarella and parmesan on top, introduce in the oven and bake at 325 degrees F for 45 minutes.

7. Cool the lasagna down, slice and serve.

Enjoy!

Lasagna Recipes with Poultry

You don't only need pork, beef or lamb to make delicious lasagnas! You can also use poultry to make the them. So, here are the best poultry lasagna recipes!

Simple Chicken and Cheese Lasagna

This is simple to make and it tastes really amazing!

Preparation Time: 10 minutes

Cooking Time: 1 hour and 10 minutes

Servings: 10

Ingredients:

- 14 ounces lasagna noodles, cooked
- 1 cup parmesan, grated
- 1 teaspoon basil, dried
- ½ cup butter, soft
- 1 teaspoon oregano, dried
- 1 yellow onion, chopped
- 1 garlic clove, minced
- A pinch of salt and black pepper
- 2 cups ricotta cheese
- ½ cup flour
- 2 cups chicken meat, cooked and shredded
- 2 cups chicken stock
- 20 ounces spinach, chopped
- 1 and ½ cups milk
- 1 tablespoon parsley, chopped
- 4 cups mozzarella cheese, shredded

Method:

1. Heat up a pot with the butter over medium heat, add the garlic and the onion, stir and cook for 3-4 minutes.

2. Add salt, pepper and the flour and stir well.

3. Add the milk and the stock, stir, cook for 1 minutes more and take off the heat.

4. Add half of the mozzarella and half of the parmesan, oregano and basil and stir well again.

5. Spread 1/3 of this mix on the bottom of a baking dish, layer, 1/3 of the lasagna noodles, the chicken and the ricotta.

6. Arrange 1/3 of the remaining lasagna noodles, then 1/3 of the sauce, the spinach, the rest of the parmesan and the rest of the mozzarella.

7. Top with the rest of the lasagna noodles, spread the rest of the sauce, sprinkle the parsley, bake at 375 degrees F for 40 minutes, cool down, slice and serve.

Enjoy!

Easy Chicken Lasagna

It's a fantastic dish!

Preparation Time: 10 minutes

Cooking Time: 1 hour and 15 minutes

Servings: 6

Ingredients:

- 12 ounces lasagna noodles, cooked
- 8 ounces cream cheese, soft
- 3 chicken breast halves, skinless and boneless
- 1 cup chicken bouillon
- 26 ounces spaghetti sauce
- 2 cups mozzarella, shredded
- ¼ cup hot water

Method:

1. Put the chicken in a pot, add water to cover, bring to a boil over medium heat, cook for 20 minutes, drain and shred.

2. In a bowl, mix the chicken bouillon with the hot water and whisk.

3. Add the chicken, half of the mozzarella and the cream cheese and stir everything,

4. Spread 1/3 of the spaghetti sauce on the bottom of a baking dish, add half of the chicken mix, then half of the lasagna noodles.

5. Repeat the layers one more time and spread the rest of the spaghetti sauce at the end.

6. Sprinkle the rest of the mozzarella, introduce in the oven, bake at 375 degrees F for 45 minutes, cool down, slice and serve.

Enjoy!

Light Chicken Lasagna

You have got to try this dish! It's so delightful!

Preparation Time: 10 minutes

Cooking Time: 2 hours and 20 minutes

Servings: 10

Ingredients:

- 16 ounces lasagna noodles, cooked
- 1 yellow onion, chopped
- 2 tablespoons olive oil
- 2 carrots, chopped
- 2 celery sticks, chopped
- 2 garlic cloves, minced
- 1 pound chicken meat, ground
- 27 ounces tomato puree
- ¼ cup tomato paste
- 2 teaspoons sugar
- 1 teaspoon oregano, dried
- 4 basil leaves, chopped
- ¾ cup white wine
- A pinch of salt and black pepper
- For the béchamel:
- ½ stick butter
- 1/3 cup flour
- 2 and ¼ cups milk
- A pinch of nutmeg, ground
- 1 cup parmesan, grated

Method:

1. Heat up a pot with the oil over medium heat, add the carrots, celery, garlic and onion, stir and cook for 5-6 minutes.

2. Add the chicken, stir and cook for another 5 minutes.

3. Add tomato puree, tomato paste, sugar, wine, oregano, basil, salt and pepper, stir and cook over medium low heat for 1 hour and 30 minutes.

4. Meanwhile, heat up a pan with the butter over medium heat, add the flour, salt, pepper, nutmeg and the milk, whisk well, cook for a couple of minutes more and take off the heat.

5. Spread a layer of the chicken mix on the bottom of a baking dish, add a layer of the béchamel sauce, then a layer of lasagna noodles.

6. Repeat with the layers until you finish the ingredients, sprinkle the parmesan on top, cover the dish with tin foul, bake at 375 degrees F for 25 minutes, uncover and cook for 25 minutes more.

7. Cool the lasagna down, slice and serve.

Enjoy!

Delicious Chicken Lasagna

This is truly delicious and easy to make!

Preparation Time: 10 minutes

Cooking Time: 1 hour and 30 minutes

Servings: 10

Ingredients:

- 42 ounces marinara sauce
- 14 ounces ricotta cheese
- 16 ounces lasagna noodles, cooked
- 2 cups rotisserie chicken, cooked and shredded
- 4 cups mozzarella cheese, shredded
- 2 tablespoons butter
- 1 cup panko bread crumbs
- ½ cup parmesan, grated

Method:

1. Spread 1 cup marinara sauce on the bottom of a baking dish, add a layer of lasagna noodles, add 1/3 of the ricotta cheese, 1/3 of the chicken, 1 cup of the mozzarella and top with 1 cup of marinara sauce.

2. Repeat the action again with the rest of the ingredients, cover the dish with tin foil, bake at 360 degrees F for 45 minutes, uncover it, sprinkle the bread crumbs on top, cook for 20 minutes more, cool down, slice and serve.

Enjoy!

Turkey Lasagna

You have to make this for your family tonight!

Preparation Time: 10 minutes

Cooking Time: 1 hour

Servings: 8

Ingredients:

- 16 ounces whole wheat lasagna noodles, cooked
- A pinch of salt and black pepper
- ¼ teaspoon garlic powder
- ½ cup yellow onion, chopped
- 6 cups spinach, torn
- 1 teaspoon olive oil
- 1 pound turkey breast, ground
- ¼ teaspoon nutmeg, ground
- 2 cups ricotta cheese
- 3 cups tomato sauce
- 2 cups mozzarella cheese, shredded
- ½ cup mushrooms, chopped
- 2 tablespoons Italian seasoning

Method:

1. Heat up a pan with the oil over medium heat, add the onion, stir and sauté for 2 minutes.

2. Add the meat, stir and cook for 7 minutes more.

3. Add salt, pepper, mushrooms, tomato sauce, Italian seasoning and the garlic powder, stir, cook for 3 minutes more and take off the heat.

4. In a bowl, mix the ricotta with the nutmeg and the spinach and stir.

5. Layer 3 lasagna noodles on the bottom of a baking dish, then spread 1/3 of the ricotta cheese, then add 1/3 of the turkey mix and 1/3 of the mozzarella.

6. Repeat the layers until you finish the ingredients, top with the remaining mozzarella, bake at 375 degrees F for 30 minutes, cool down, slice and serve.

Enjoy!

Turkey and Zucchinis Lasagna

This is so hearty and rich!

Preparation Time: 10 minutes

Cooking Time: 50 minutes

Servings: 10

Ingredients:

- 16 ounces lasagna noodles, cooked
- 2 garlic cloves, minced
- 1 yellow onion, chopped
- 1 tablespoon olive oil
- 3 zucchinis, chopped
- 12 ounces turkey meat, ground
- A pinch of salt and black pepper
- 28 ounces canned tomatoes, crushed
- 6 ounces tomato paste
- ¼ cup parmesan, grated
- 1 tablespoon Italian seasoning
- 14 ounces ricotta
- 10 ounces spinach, chopped
- 1 egg, whisked
- 2 and ½ cups mozzarella, shredded
- 2 tablespoons cilantro, chopped

Method:

1. Heat up a pan with the oil over medium heat, add the zucchinis, onion, garlic, salt and pepper, stir and sauté for 4 minutes.

2. Add the turkey, stir and cook for 5 minutes.

3. Add Italian seasoning, tomato paste and tomatoes, stir, simmer for 10 minutes and take off the heat.

4. In a bowl, mix the ricotta with the spinach, egg and the parmesan and whisk.

5. Spoon a layer of the zucchinis and meat on the bottom of the baking dish, add a layer of lasagna noodles and a layer of spinach.

6. Continue with the layers until you finish the ingredients, sprinkle the mozzarella and the cilantro on top, bake at 350 degrees F for 45 minutes, cool down, slice and serve.

Enjoy!

Turkey and Sweet Potato Lasagna

Everyone will love this!

Preparation Time: 10 minutes

Cooking Time: 45 minutes

Servings: 4

Ingredients:

- 1 and ½ pounds turkey meat, ground
- 1 pound sweet potato, thinly sliced
- ½ cup cottage cheese
- 1 egg white, whisked
- ½ cup mozzarella, shredded
- 2 tomatoes, chopped
- 15 ounces tomato sauce
- 1/3 cup red onion, chopped
- 1/3 cup mushrooms, sliced
- 1 tablespoon garlic paste
- ½ cup cilantro, chopped

Method:

1. In a bowl, mix the cottage cheese with the egg white and whisk.

2. Heat up a pan over medium heat, add the onions, garlic paste, the turkey meat, tomatoes, cilantro, mushrooms and tomato sauce, stir, cook for 10 minutes more and take off the heat.

3. Spread a layer of sweet potato slices on the bottom of a baking dish, add a layer of meat sauce and then a layer of cottage cheese.

4. Continue with the rest of the ingredients, top with the mozzarella and the cilantro, bake the lasagna in the oven at 370 degrees F for 45 minutes, cool down, slice and serve.

Enjoy!

Duck Lasagna

It's a special autumn dish!

Preparation Time: 10 minutes

Cooking Time: 2 hours and 20 minutes

Servings: 12

Ingredients:

- 5 pounds duck, quartered
- 3 and ½ pounds tomatoes, peeled and crushed
- 4 garlic cloves, minced
- 2 yellow onions, chopped
- 4 carrots, chopped
- 2 cups white wine
- 2 celery stalks, chopped
- 2 cups tomato paste
- 1 bunch marjoram, chopped
- 2 cups pecorino, grated
- 16 ounces lasagna sheets
- A pinch of salt and black pepper
- 2 tablespoons olive oil

Method:

1. Heat up a pot with the oil over medium heat, add the onions and the garlic, stir and cook for 5 minutes.

2. Add the celery, the carrots and the tomatoes, stir, bring to a simmer and cook for 20 minutes.

3. Add the duck, the wine, tomato paste, salt and pepper, stir and simmer for 1 hour.

4. Shred the meat, discard bones and stir the mix one more time.

5. Spread a layer of meat sauce on the bottom of a baking dish, and then add a layer of lasagna noodles and 1/3 of the pecorino cheese.

6. Continue with the layers until you finish all the ingredients, top with a layer of pecorino, sprinkle the marjoram, bake the lasagna at 375 degrees F for 45 minutes, cool down, slice and serve.

Enjoy!

Duck and Wine Lasagna

It's an elegant combination!

Preparation Time: 10 minutes

Cooking Time: 3 hours

Servings: 6

Ingredients:

- 3 tablespoons olive oil
- 4 duck legs
- 4 leeks, chopped
- 1 carrot, chopped
- 2 garlic cloves, minced
- 4 prosciutto slices, chopped
- ½ teaspoon cloves, ground
- 3 rosemary springs, chopped
- 7 sage leaves, chopped
- 1 cup red wine
- 1 cup chicken stock
- 30 ounces canned tomatoes, chopped
- A pinch of salt and black pepper
- 1 pound lasagna sheets, cooked
- 2 cups parmesan, grated
- 4 tablespoons butter
- 3 tablespoons flour
- 2 cups milk

Method:

1. Heat up a pot with the oil over medium high heat, add the garlic, leeks and carrots, stir and cook for 7 minutes.

2. Add the duck, toss and brown for 7 minutes more.

3. Add the prosciutto, cloves, rosemary, sage, tomatoes, stock and wine, bring to a simmer and cook for 1 hour and 30 minutes.

4. Shred the meat, discard bones and stir the mix one more time.

5. Heat up a pan with the milk over medium high heat, add the flour and the butter, whisk well, cook until it thickens and take off the heat.

6. Spread a layer of the duck sauce on the bottom of a baking dish, and then add a layer of lasagna noodles, then continue with a layer of béchamel and a layer of parmesan.

7. Continue the layers until you finish all the ingredients, top with parmesan, bake at 370 degrees F for 1 hour, cool down, slice and serve.

Enjoy!

Duck and Mushroom Lasagna

We can guarantee you will ask for more!

Preparation Time: 10 minutes

Cooking Time: 2 hours and 30 minutes

Servings: 12

Ingredients:

- 4 duck legs
- 3 tablespoons olive oil
- 2 tablespoons butter
- 1 yellow onion, chopped
- 1 celery stalk, chopped
- 1 carrot, chopped
- 2 tablespoons red wine
- A pinch of cinnamon powder
- 4 thyme springs, chopped
- 4 tomatoes, chopped
- 12 ounces chicken stock
- 6 shallots, chopped
- A pinch of salt and black pepper
- 1 cup parmesan, grated
- 2 leeks, chopped
- 1 cup mushrooms, chopped
- 1 and ½ cups béchamel sauce
- 16 ounces lasagna noodles, cooked

Method:

1. Heat up a pot with the oil and the butter over medium heat, add the onion, carrots, shallots, cinnamon, salt, pepper, celery, leeks, mushrooms, thyme and tomatoes, stir and sauté for 10 minutes.

2. Add the duck legs, toss, brown for 10 minutes more, take off the heat, add the stock and the wine, introduce in the oven and bake at 360 degrees F for 1 hour.

3. Shred the meat, discard bones and mix the whole thing again.

4. Spread a layer of the duck sauce on the bottom of a baking dish, continue with a layer of lasagna noodles and a layer of béchamel sauce.

5. Continue the layers until you finish all the ingredients, sprinkle the parmesan on top, bake at 360 degrees F for 1 more hour, cool the lasagna down, slice and serve.

Enjoy!

Lasagna Recipes with Fish and Seafood

Now it's time for you to try something completely new! It's time for you to try some of the best lasagna recipes with fish and seafood! They are so incredible and amazing!

Simple Fish Lasagna

It's a simple recipe!

Preparation Time: 10 minutes

Cooking Time: 50 minutes

Servings: 6

Ingredients:

- 1 pound haddock fillet, skinless, boneless
- 15 ounces skimmed milk
- 1 bay leaf
- 1 thyme spring
- 2 tablespoons butter
- 2 tablespoons flour
- 2 cups cheddar cheese, shredded
- 12 ounces lasagna sheets, cooked
- 2 carrots, sliced
- 1 cup baby spinach, torn
- A pinch of salt and black pepper

Method:

1. Put the fish in a pot, add the milk, bay leaf and thyme, bring to a simmer, cook over medium heat for 3 minutes, strain the milk into a bowl, flake the fish and put it in another one.

2. Heat up a pan with the butter over medium heat, add the flour, whisk well for 1-2 minutes, add the milk, whisk again, bring to a simmer, cook until it thickens, take off the heat and mix with 1/3 of the cheese.

3. Pour a layer of this sauce into a baking dish, add a layer of lasagna sheets, add a layer of fish, spinach and carrots and top with another layer of lasagna.

4. Repeat the action with the rest of the ingredients, sprinkle the rest of the cheese on top, bake at 360 degrees F for 25 minutes, cool down, slice and serve.

Enjoy!

Seafood Lasagna

It's time for something really amazing: a seafood lasagna!

Preparation Time: 10 minutes

Cooking Time: 40 minutes

Servings: 10

Ingredients:

- 2 tablespoons olive oil
- 1 green onion, chopped
- ½ cup butter+ 2 tablespoon
- 8 ounces crabmeat, chopped
- ½ cup white flour
- A pinch of salt and black pepper
- ½ cup chicken stock
- 8 ounces clam juice
- 1 and ½ cups milk
- 1 pound bay scallops
- 1 cup heavy cream
- 1 pound shrimp, peeled, deveined
- ½ cup parmesan, grated
- 14 ounces lasagna noodles, cooked

Method:

1. Heat up a pan with the oil over medium heat, add the onion and 2 tablespoons butter, stir and sauté for 2 minutes.

2. Add the clam juice and the stock and stir.

3. Add shrimp, crabmeat, scallops, salt and pepper, stir, simmer for 5 minutes, drain the seafood into a bowl and reserve the cooking liquid.

4. Heat up another pan with the rest of the butter over medium heat, add the flour, milk and the reserved cooking liquid, whisk well, simmer for 2 minutes, take off the heat, add ¼ cup of cheese and the heavy cream and whisk.

5. Mix the seafood with ¾ cup of the white mixture you've just made and stir.

6. Spread ½ cup of the white sauce on the bottom of a baking dish, layer 3 lasagna noodles, spread ½ of the seafood mix and 1 and ¼ cups white sauce.

7. Repeat the action with the rest of the ingredients, top with the remaining cheese, bake at 370 degrees F for 40 minutes, cool down, slice and serve.

Enjoy!

Fish and Zucchini Lasagna

You have got to try this special dish right away!

Preparation Time: 10 minutes

Cooking Time: 50 minutes

Servings: 6

Ingredients:

- 9 ounces lasagna sheets, cooked
- 1 cod fillet, skinless and boneless
- 4 zucchinis, chopped
- 2 tablespoons olive oil+ a drizzle
- 1 pound tomatoes, peeled and crushed
- 1 pint tomato coulis
- 5 ounces parmesan, grated
- 2 shallots, chopped
- 8 basil leaves, chopped
- 2 garlic cloves, minced
- 1 tablespoons sugar
- A pinch of salt and black pepper

Method:

1. Heat up a pan with a drizzle of oil over medium heat, add the fish, cook for 2 minutes on each side, season with salt and pepper, take off the heat, cool down and shred.

2. Heat up a pan with 2 tablespoons oil over medium heat, add the garlic and the shallots, stir and sauté for 3 minutes.

3. Add the zucchini, tomatoes, sugar, salt and pepper, toss and cook for 12-13 minutes.

4. Add half of the tomato couli, cook for 15 minutes and take off the heat.

5. Add half of the parmesan and the basil and stir once more.

6. Arrange a layer of lasagna sheets on the bottom of a baking dish, spread the zucchini, the fish and cover with the rest of the lasagna sheets.

7. Spread the rest of the tomato couli and the rest of the parmesan, bake at 375 degrees F for 25 minutes, cool down, slice and serve.

Enjoy!

Fish and Green Pea Lasagna

This tastes divine!

Preparation Time: 10 minutes

Cooking Time: 50 minutes

Servings: 6

Ingredients:

- 4 cups peas
- 1 and ¼ cup chicken stock
- A pinch of salt and black pepper
- 1 yellow onion, chopped
- ¼ cup butter, soft
- 1/3 cup white flour
- 2 cups milk
- ½ cup parmesan, grated
- 2 garlic cloves, minced
- 14 ounces lasagna noodles, cooked
- ¼ cup breadcrumbs
- 1 and ½ pounds white fish fillets, boneless, skinless and cubed
- 2 cups mozzarella, shredded

Method:

1. In a blender, mix the peas with ¼ cup stock, salt and pepper, pulse and transfer to a bowl.

2. Heat up a pan with the butter over medium heat, add the garlic and the onion, stir and cook for 3-5 minutes.

3. Add the flour and whisk well.

4. Add the rest of the stock, the milk, salt and pepper, whisk well, cook for a couple more minutes and take off the heat.

5. In a bowl, mix the parmesan with the breadcrumbs and stir.

6. Spread ¼ of the béchamel sauce you've made on the bottom of a baking dish, add a layer of lasagna noodles and continue with half of the fish.

7. Add ¼ more sauce, then continue with another layer of lasagna noodles and spread the peas puree.

8. Spread the mozzarella, add another layer of lasagna noodles and then arrange the rest of the fish.

9. Add ¼ of the remaining béchamel, then layer the rest of the lasagna noodles and the rest of the béchamel at the end.

10. Sprinkle the parmesan mix at the end, bake the lasagna at 350 degrees F for 40 minutes, cool down, slice and serve.

Enjoy!

Mixed Seafood Lasagna

This will be the star of your next meal!

Preparation Time: 10 minutes

Cooking Time: 50 minutes

Servings: 6

Ingredients:

- 15 ounces milk
- 1 garlic clove, minced
- 2 bay leaves
- 2 ounces butter, melted
- 1 teaspoon mustard
- 2 ounces white flour
- A pinch of salt and black pepper
- 14 ounces no-cook lasagna noodles
- 2 tablespoons tarragon, chopped
- 14 ounces mixed salmon, cod and mussels, chopped
- A handful spinach, chopped
- 5 ounces cheddar, grated
- 3 ounces parmesan, grated

Method:

1. Put the milk in a pot, heat up over medium heat, add the bay leaves and the garlic, stir and bring to a simmer.

2. Heat up a pot with the butter over medium heat, add the flour, whisk for 2 minutes and take off the heat.

3. Discard bay leaves from the milk, add to pan with the butter and whisk well.

4. Add salt, pepper and the mustard, whisk well again and leave aside.

5. In a bowl, mix fish, seafood, tarragon and spinach with some of the sauce and stir.

6. Spread a layer of sauce on the bottom of a baking dish, add a layer of lasagna noodles, then add a layer of fish sauce and top with another layer of lasagna sauce.

7. Continue with the layers until you finish all the ingredients, sprinkle the cheddar and the parmesan, bake at 360 degrees F for 40 minutes, cool down a bit, slice and serve.

Enjoy!

Seafood and Mushrooms Lasagna

Get ready to taste something exceptional!

Preparation Time: 10 minutes

Cooking Time: 1 hour

Servings: 4

Ingredients:

- 2 teaspoons olive oil
- 1 pound mushrooms, chopped
- 2 tablespoons thyme, chopped
- 1 and ½ cups onion, chopped
- ¼ cup white wine
- 2 garlic cloves, minced
- 13 ounces canned crabmeat, drained
- 1 pound shrimp, peeled, deveined and halved
- 2 cups fish stock
- A pinch of salt and black pepper
- 5 ounces goat cheese, crumbled
- 1 cup cottage cheese
- 1 tablespoon lemon juice
- ¼ cup basil, chopped
- ¼ cup white flour
- 1 garlic clove, minced
- 1 cup milk
- ¼ cup parmesan, grated
- 8 ounces lasagna noodles, cooked
- 2 cups mozzarella, shredded
- ¼ cup parsley, chopped

Method:

1. Heat up a pot with the oil over medium heat, add onion, mushrooms, thyme, salt, pepper and the garlic, stir and sauté for 10 minutes.

2. Add the wine, boil for 2 minutes more, take off the heat, add crabmeat and stir.

3. In a bowl, mix the goat cheese with basil, cottage cheese and lemon juice and stir.

4. Heat up a pot with the milk over medium heat, add the flour and the shrimp stock, whisk well, bring to a simmer, cook for 5 minutes, take off the heat and mix with the parmesan.

5. Spread ½ cup of this mix on the bottom of a baking dish, arrange 4 lasagna noodles over it, add 1/3 of the goat cheese mix, 1/3 of the crab and mushroom mix, also add 1/3 of the shrimp, 2/3 cup of the milk sauce and 2/3 cup mozzarella.

6. Repeat the layers, top with the remaining mozzarella, sprinkle the parsley on top, bake at 375 degrees F for 40 minutes, cool down a bit, slice and serve.

Enjoy!

Salmon Lasagna

This is one of our favorite lasagna recipes!

Preparation Time: 10 minutes

Cooking Time: 1 hour

Servings: 6

Ingredients:

- 2 pounds salmon, skinless and boneless
- 1 teaspoon olive oil
- A pinch of salt and black pepper
- 5 tablespoons butter
- 5 tablespoons flour
- 3 cups warm milk
- 1 tablespoon dill, chopped
- Juice of 1 lemon
- 2 teaspoons mustard
- ¼ cup gruyere cheese, grated
- 6 ounces asparagus, halved
- 14 ounces no-boil lasagna sheets
- 2 cups mozzarella, shredded

Method:

1. Place the salmon in a baking dish, season with salt and pepper, drizzle the oil, cover with tin foil, bake at 350 degrees F for 15 minutes, flake and put in a bowl.

2. In a pot, mix the butter with the milk, dill and flour, whisk well and cook over medium heat until the béchamel sauce thickens.

3. Add lemon juice, gruyere cheese, mustard, salt and pepper, whisk really well and take off the heat.

4. Arrange 3 lasagna noodles on the bottom of a baking dish, add 1/3 of the béchamel sauce and spread the asparagus.

5. Add half of the mozzarella, then layer 3 more lasagna noodles and 1/3 of the béchamel.

6. Arrange the salmon, then layer the rest of the lasagna noodles and spread the rest of the béchamel on top.

7. Sprinkle the rest of the mozzarella, bake at 360 degrees F for 30 minutes, cool down, slice and serve.

Enjoy!

Salmon and Spinach Lasagna

You have to try this combination! It's the best!

Preparation Time: 10 minutes

Cooking Time: 1 hour and 10 minutes

Servings: 5

Ingredients:

- 8 ounces lasagna sheets, cooked
- 1 tablespoon olive oil
- 1 yellow onion, chopped
- 2 garlic cloves, minced
- 1 pound salmon fillets, boneless
- 1 pound spinach, torn
- 1 cup white wine
- A pinch of salt and black pepper
- 2 tablespoons butter
- 2 tablespoons white flour
- 2 cups single cream
- ½ teaspoon nutmeg, ground
- 4 ounces mozzarella, shredded

Method:

1. Heat up a pan with the oil over medium heat, add the onion and sauté for 5 minutes.

2. Shred the salmon, add it to the pan, also add the garlic, spinach, wine, salt and pepper, toss, cook for 6-7 minutes more and take off the heat.

3. Heat up another pan with the butter over medium heat, add the flour and whisk well.

4. Also add the cream, some salt, pepper and the nutmeg, whisk well, cook until it thickens and also take off the heat.

5. Spoon 1/3 of the salmon mix on the bottom of a baking dish, layer 1/3 of the white sauce you've made and top with 2 lasagna noodles.

6. Repeat the action with the rest of the ingredients, cover the dish with tin foil, bake at 360 degrees F for 30 minutes, uncover the dish, bake for 10 minutes more, cool down, slice and serve.

Enjoy!

Healthy Fish Lasagna

Everyone can make this great dish!

Preparation Time: 10 minutes

Cooking Time: 1 hour

Servings: 8

Ingredients:

- 3 tablespoons olive oil
- ¼ cup white flour
- 3 cups milk
- ¼ cup parmesan, grated
- A pinch of salt and black pepper
- 10 ounces spinach, torn
- 2 cups mozzarella, shredded
- 1 cup ricotta cheese
- 16 ounces lasagna noodles, cooked
- 10 ounces canned salmon, drained and flaked
- 1 tomato, chopped

Method:

1. Heat up a pan with the oil over medium heat, add the flour, whisk and cook for 1 minute.

2. Add the milk, the parmesan, a pinch of salt and pepper, whisk well, cook until the sauce thickens and take off the heat.

3. In a bowl, mix the spinach with the ricotta and mozzarella and stir.

4. Spread ½ cup white sauce on the bottom of a baking dish, arrange 1/3 of the lasagna noodles, spoon half of the ricotta mix and half of the salmon as well.

5. Repeat the layers again, top with the rest of the lasagna noodles and white sauce, cover the dish with tin foil, bake at 360 degrees F for 45 minutes, cool the lasagna, sprinkle the tomato all over, slice and serve.

Enjoy!

Crab and Shrimp Lasagna

It's a delicious dish for you to prepare for your loved ones!

Preparation Time: 10 minutes

Cooking Time: 1 hour

Servings: 8

Ingredients:

- ¼ cup flour
- 14 ounces lasagna noodles, cooked
- ¼ cup butter
- 1 yellow onion, chopped
- 2 cups half and half
- 2 garlic cloves, minced
- 1 cup chicken stock
- A pinch of salt and black pepper
- 1/3 cup dry sherry
- 1 egg, whisked
- ½ cup parmesan, grated
- 15 ounces ricotta cheese
- ¼ cup parsley
- 16 ounces crabmeat, chopped
- 8 ounces shrimp, cooked, peeled and deveined

Method:

1. Heat up a pan with the butter over medium heat, add the garlic and the onion, stir and sauté for 3 minutes.

2. Add the flour, half and half, stock, salt, pepper and the sherry, whisk well, cook for 1-2 minutes more and take off the heat.

3. In a bowl, mix the parmesan with the egg, ricotta and the parsley and stir.

4. Spread ¾ cup of the sauce on the bottom of a baking dish, layer 3 lasagna noodles, spread half of the crabmeat and half of the shrimp, then spread ¾ cup of the sauce and sprinkle half of the mozzarella.

5. Repeat the action until you finish all the ingredients, sprinkle the rest of the mozzarella at the end, bake the lasagna at 350 degrees F for 45 minutes, cool down a bit, slice and serve.

Enjoy!

Shrimp Lasagna

This is a flavored and rich lasagna!

Preparation Time: 10 minutes

Cooking Time: 1 hour

Servings: 8

Ingredients:

- 1 red bell pepper, chopped
- 1 tablespoon olive oil
- 1 yellow onion, chopped
- 2 celery stalks, chopped
- 3 tablespoons Cajun seasoning
- 28 ounces canned tomatoes, crushed
- 6 ounces tomato paste
- 2 teaspoons sugar
- 4 ounces cheddar cheese, shredded
- 4 ounces jack cheese, shredded
- 4 ounces mozzarella, shredded
- 16 ounces ricotta cheese
- 1 cup parmesan, grated
- 2 eggs, whisked
- 1 pound shrimp, peeled, deveined and chopped
- 1 pound lasagna noodles, cooked

Method:

1. Heat up a pan with the oil over medium high heat, add the bell pepper, onion and celery, stir and cook for 5 minutes.

2. Add the garlic, 1 tablespoon Cajun seasoning, tomatoes, tomato paste and sugar, stir, bring to a simmer and cook for 15 minutes.

3. In a bowl, mix the cheddar with the jack cheese and mozzarella and stir.

4. In another bowl, mix the parmesan with the ricotta, eggs, the rest of the Cajun seasoning and a handful of the cheese mix you've just made and stir.

5. Spread a layer of the tomatoes sauce on the bottom of a baking dish, then layer some lasagna noodles and 1/3 of the remaining sauce.

6. Add a layer of shrimp, spread a layer of ricotta mix and sprinkle some of the mixed cheese.

7. Repeat the layers until you finish all the ingredients, top with the remaining shredded cheese, cover with tin foil, bake at 375 degrees F for 40 minutes, remove the foil, cook the lasagna for 20 minutes more, cool down, slice and serve.

Enjoy!

Shrimp and Broccoli Lasagna

This is delicious and healthy at the same time!

Preparation Time: 10 minutes

Cooking Time: 1 hour

Servings: 6

Ingredients:

- 1 pound broccoli florets, chopped
- 9 ounces lasagna noodles, cooked
- 3 tablespoons butter
- ¼ cup flour
- ¼ cup green onions, chopped
- ¼ teaspoon mustard powder
- A pinch of salt and black pepper
- ¼ teaspoon thyme, dried
- 2 and ½ cups milk
- 4 ounces Monterey Jack cheese, shredded
- 2 and ½ cups cheddar cheese, shredded
- 1 pound shrimp, cooked, peeled and deveined

Method:

1. Heat up a pan with the butter over medium heat, add onions, mustard powder, salt, pepper, thyme and the flour, stir well and cook for a couple of minutes

2. Add the milk, whisk well, cook until the mixture thickens, take off the heat, add the Monterey Jack cheese and whisk well.

3. Spread ½ cup of this mix on the bottom of a baking dish, then layer 3 lasagna noodles, the broccoli, ½ cup cheddar and 1 more cup of sauce.

4. Add the rest of the lasagna noodles, then add the shrimp, 1 cup cheddar, the rest of the sauce and the rest of the cheese.

5. Bake the lasagna at 350 degrees F for 35 minutes, cool it down a bit, slice and serve.

Enjoy!

Shrimp and Tomato Lasagna

Here's a new lasagna idea! Try it right away!

Preparation Time: 10 minutes

Cooking Time: 55 minutes

Servings: 12

Ingredients:

- 4 cups tomato sauce
- 1 yellow onion, chopped
- 1 tablespoon butter
- 5 garlic cloves, minced
- 10 ounces spinach, torn
- 1 and ½ pounds shrimp, peeled, deveined and chopped
- ¾ cup heavy cream
- 14 ounces ricotta cheese
- A pinch of salt and black pepper
- 3 eggs, whisked
- 16 ounces lasagna noodles, cooked
- ½ cup parmesan, grated

Method:

1. Heat up a pan with the butter over medium high heat, add the onion, stir and sauté for 5 minutes.

2. Add the garlic and spinach, toss, cook for 4-5 minutes more and take off the heat.

3. Add the shrimp and the cream and stir.

4. In a bowl, mix the ricotta with the eggs, salt and pepper, stir well, add to the shrimp mix and toss everything.

5. Spread 1 cup of tomato sauce on the bottom of a baking dish, arrange 4 lasagna noodles over it and spread half of the shrimp sauce.

6. Layer 4 more lasagna noodles, then spread ¾ cup tomato sauce and the rest of the shrimp.

7. Top with the rest of the lasagna noodles, the rest of the tomato sauce and the parmesan.

8. Bake this at 375 degrees F for 45 minutes, cool down, slice and serve.

Enjoy!

Great Italian Shrimp Lasagna

Try an Italian style lasagna for a change!

Preparation Time: 10 minutes

Cooking Time: 50 minutes

Servings: 10

Ingredients:

- ¼ cup flour
- A pinch of salt and black pepper
- ¼ cup butter, soft
- ½ cup of celery, chopped
- ½ cups carrots, chopped
- 2 garlic cloves, minced
- 1 and 1/3 cups chicken stock
- 2 cups half and half
- 1 egg, whisked
- 15 ounces ricotta cheese
- 14 ounces no-boil lasagna noodles
- ½ cup parmesan, grated
- 12 ounces packed scampi, heated up
- 12 ounces shrimp, cooked, peeled and deveined
- 3 cups mozzarella, shredded
- 1 teaspoon parsley flakes

Method:

1. Heat up a pot with the butter over medium heat, add the celery, garlic and carrots, stir and cook for 5 minutes.

2. Add the flour, salt, pepper, half and half and the stock, whisk well, boil until it thickens, and take off the heat.

3. In a bowl, mix the parmesan with the ricotta and the egg and stir.

4. Spread ¾ cup of the sauce on the bottom of a baking dish, layer 3 lasagna noodles, continue with half of the scampi and half of the shrimp and then spread ¾ cup of sauce.

5. Sprinkle 1 cup of mozzarella, then layer 3 more lasagna noodles and spread the ricotta mix.

6. Layer ¾ cup of sauce, 1 more cup of mozzarella and top with 3 more lasagna noodles.

7. Spread the rest of the shrimp, scampi and the mozzarella, sprinkle the parsley, bake the lasagna at 350 degrees F for 40 minutes, cool it down a bit, slice and serve.

Enjoy!

Shrimp and Lobster Lasagna

This is a fancy lasagna you should really try!

Preparation Time: 10 minutes

Cooking Time: 50 minutes

Servings: 10

Ingredients:

- 15 ounces ricotta cheese
- 2 eggs, whisked
- 1 cup mozzarella, shredded
- 2 cups cheddar cheese, shredded
- 2 tablespoons parsley, chopped
- A pinch of salt and black pepper
- 22 ounces Alfredo sauce
- 20 ounces no-boil lasagna noodles
- 2 pounds lobster meat, cooked and chopped
- 10 ounces baby spinach
- 1 yellow onion, chopped
- 1 tablespoon garlic, minced

Method:

1. In a bowl, mix the ricotta with half of the cheddar, eggs, half of the mozzarella, half of the parmesan, garlic, onion, parsley, salt and pepper and stir.

2. Spread 1 and ½ cups Alfredo sauce on the bottom of a baking dish, add a layer of lasagna noodles, then 1/3 of the lobster meat, 1/3 ricotta cheese, 1/3 spinach mix and another layer of Alfredo sauce.

3. Repeat the action until you finish all the ingredients, sprinkle the rest of the cheddar, mozzarella and parmesan at the end.

4. Cover the baking dish with tin foil, bake at 350 degrees F for 45 minutes, cool it down a bit, slice and serve.

Enjoy!

Vegan Lasagna Recipes

Trust us! These are going to be real culinary feasts! You will simply adore these next lasagna recipes! Try them all really soon and see what we mean!

Tofu Lasagna

This will impress you with its amazing taste!

Preparation Time: 10 minutes

Cooking Time: 40 minutes

Servings: 10

Ingredients:

- 16 ounces lasagna noodles, cooked
- 1 tablespoon olive oil
- 8 ounces mushrooms, sliced
- 1 zucchini, chopped
- 1 cup peas
- 10 cups marinara sauce
- 12 ounces spinach, torn
- 28 ounces tofu, drained, pressed and crumbled
- 10 ounces roasted garlic hummus
- ¼ cup basil, chopped
- ½ cup nutritional yeast
- A pinch of salt and black pepper
- 1 teaspoon garlic powder

Method:

1. Heat up a pan with the oil over medium heat, add the mushrooms and the zucchini, salt and pepper, toss and sauté for 5 minutes.

2. Add the peas and the spinach, cook for 5 minutes more and take off the heat.

3. In a bowl, mix the tofu with the hummus, salt, pepper, basil, garlic powder and nutritional yeast and stir well.

4. Spread 1 and ½ cups of the marinara sauce on the bottom of a baking dish, layer 4 lasagna noodles, then spread half of the tofu mix and half of the vegetable mix.

5. Add 1 and ½ cups of marinara sauce, then another layer of lasagna noodles, tofu mix and veggies mix.

6. Top with another layer of lasagna noodles and with the rest of the marinara sauce, bake at 360 degrees F for 30 minutes, cool down a bit, slice and serve.

Enjoy!

Colored Veggie Lasagna

This looks so good! Can you imagine how great it can taste?

Preparation Time: 10 minutes

Cooking Time: 50 minutes

Servings: 6

Ingredients:

- 6 tablespoons olive oil
- 4 garlic cloves, minced
- 1 yellow onion, chopped
- 1 pound mushrooms, chopped
- 2 carrots, chopped
- 1 pound spinach, torn
- 1 zucchini, chopped
- A pinch of salt and black pepper
- 2 cups soy milk
- 1 cup veggie stock
- ½ cup flour
- 2 tablespoons nutritional yeast
- 3 cups marinara sauce
- 15 ounces lasagna noodles, cooked

Method:

1. Heat up a pan with 2 tablespoons oil over medium high heat, add the garlic and the onion, stir and sauté for a couple of minutes.

2. Add the mushrooms, stir and cook for 5 minutes more.

3. Add the zucchini, salt, pepper, carrot and spinach, toss, cook for a couple more minutes and take off the heat.

4. Heat up a pot with the rest of the oil over medium heat, add soy milk, stock and the flour, whisk well, cook for 10 minutes until it thickens and take off the heat.

5. Add the nutritional yeast, a pinch of salt and pepper and whisk.

6. Spread a layer of marinara sauce on the bottom of a baking dish, then add a layer of soy milk mixtures and a layer of lasagna noodles.

7. Add another layer of marinara sauce, then spread half of the veggies, some of the soy milk sauce and then layer more lasagna noodles.

8. Repeat with the remaining ingredients making sure you top with a layer of marinara and a layer of soy sauce mix.

9. Bake the lasagna at 400 degrees F for 25 minutes, cool it down a bit, slice and serve.

Enjoy!

Vegan Lasagna

The recipe is simply incredible!

Preparation Time: 10 minutes

Cooking Time: 1 hour

Servings: 6

Ingredients:

- 1 cup almond ricotta
- 2 tablespoons chickpea flour
- 1 cup basil, chopped
- 1 cup spinach, chopped
- 3 and ½ cups of marinara sauce
- 10 ounces cashew mozzarella, shredded
- 12 ounces lasagna noodles, cooked
- 1 cup hemp parmesan, grated

Method:

1. In your food processor, mix the almond ricotta with the chickpea flour, pulse well and transfer half of this mix to a bowl.

2. Add the basil and the spinach to the food processor, pulse well and also transfer to a bowl.

3. Spread ½ cup of marinara sauce on the bottom of a baking dish, then layer 4 lasagna noodles and the reserved ricotta mix.

4. Layer 1 more cup marinara sauce, then continue with the lasagna noodles, then spread the green almond ricotta mix and 1 cup marinara sauce.

5. Add the last layer of lasagna noodles, then add the rest of the marinara sauce and then spread the cashew mozzarella.

6. Cover the dish with tin foil, bake at 350 degrees F for 30 minutes, then uncover the dish, bake it at 400 degrees F for 14 minutes more, cool the mix down, slice and serve.

Enjoy!

Fast Vegan Lasagna

This is a fast and so delicious recipe!

Preparation Time: 10 minutes

Cooking Time: 50 minutes

Servings: 8

Ingredients:

- 27 ounces mushrooms, chopped
- 2 tablespoons soy sauce
- 40 ounces canned tomatoes, chopped
- A pinch of salt and black pepper
- 6 tablespoons olive oil
- 4 cups soy milk
- 5 tablespoons cashew flour
- 2 teaspoons mustard
- 16 ounces spinach lasagna sheets, cooked
- 2 tomatoes, thinly sliced

Method:

1. Heat up a pot with the soy sauce over medium heat, add the mushrooms, stir and sauté them for 10 minutes.

2. Add the tomatoes, salt and pepper, stir, bring to a simmer, cook for 5-6 minutes and take off the heat.

3. Heat up a pot with the oil over medium high heat, add the flour and the soy milk, whisk well, cook until the sauce thickens, take off the heat, add salt, pepper and the mustard and stir well.

4. Spread a layer of tomato and mushrooms sauce on the bottom of a baking dish, and then add a layer of lasagna sheets, a layer of tomato and mushroom sauce and a layer for white sauce.

5. Continue with the layers until you finish all the ingredients, spread a layer of tomato slices at the end, bake at 360 degrees F for 30 minutes, cool down, slice and serve.

Enjoy!

Special Veggie Lasagna

You will love this!

Preparation Time: 10 minutes

Cooking Time: 50 minutes

Servings: 8

Ingredients:

- 3 carrots, chopped
- 2 tablespoons olive oil
- 1 zucchini, chopped
- 1 green bell pepper, chopped
- A pinch of salt and black pepper
- 1 yellow onion, chopped
- 6 ounces baby spinach
- 2 cups marinara sauce
- 4 cups cashew cheese, grated
- 14 ounces no-boil lasagna sheets

Method:

1. Heat up a pan with the oil over medium heat, add the bell pepper, the carrots, zucchini, onion, salt and pepper, toss and cook for 10 minutes.

2. Add the spinach, stir and cook for 3 minutes more.

3. In a bowl, mix half of the cashew cheese with the veggies mix and stir well.

4. Spread ½ cup of marinara sauce on the bottom of a baking dish, layer 3 lasagna noodles, then spread half of the veggies mix, ¾ cup marinara sauce and ½ cup cashew cheese.

5. Repeat the action with the rest of the ingredients, top with the remaining cheese, bake at 360 degrees F for 35 minutes, cool down, slice and serve.

Enjoy!

Zucchini Lasagna

This is simply amazing and rich!

Preparation Time: 10 minutes

Cooking Time: 35 minutes

Servings: 6

Ingredients:

- 1 garlic clove, minced
- 8 scallions, chopped
- 1 tablespoon olive oil
- A pinch of salt and black pepper
- 1 carrot, cut into long strips
- 1 zucchini, cut into long strips
- 2 and ½ cups spinach, torn
- 2 cups tomato and basil sauce
- 1 and ½ cups cashew cheese, shredded
- 15 ounces lasagna sheets, cooked

Method:

1. Heat up a pan with the oil over medium heat, add the garlic and stir it for 1 minute.

2. Add the scallions, salt and pepper, stir and sauté for 2 minutes.

3. Add the zucchini and the carrots, stir and cook for 5 more minutes.

4. Add the spinach, toss and take off the heat.

5. Spread a layer of lasagna sheets on the bottom of a baking dish, add 1/3 of the veggies, ¼ of the tomato sauce and ¼ of the cashew cheese.

6. Repeat the action until you finish all the ingredients, top with the remaining cheese, bake at 350 degrees F for 25 minutes, cool down, slice and serve.

Enjoy!

Carrot Lasagna

This should be a real culinary experience!

Preparation Time: 10 minutes

Cooking Time: 30 minutes

Servings: 4

Ingredients:

- 12 ounces semolina lasagna noodles, cooked
- 2 carrots, peeled and sliced
- A pinch of salt and black pepper
- 1 cup kale, torn
- 1 garlic clove, minced
- 1 tablespoon flaxmeal mixed with 2 tablespoons water
- 1 tablespoon olive oil
- 1 cup cashew cheese, shredded
- ¼ cup water
- 1 and ½ cups tomato sauce
- 1 red onion, chopped

Method:

1. In a bowl, mix half of the cashew cheese with flaxmeal, salt, pepper and kale and stir well.

2. Heat up a pan with the oil over medium high heat, add the garlic and the onion, toss and cook for 2-3 minutes.

3. Add the zucchini, carrots, water and tomato sauce, stir and cook for 10 minutes more.

4. Pour 1/3 of the zucchini sauce on the bottom of a baking dish, layer 3 lasagna noodles, then add the kale milk and sprinkle half of the remaining cashew cheese.

5. Repeat the action with the rest of the zucchini sauce and lasagna noodles, top with the rest of the cashew cheese, cover the dish with tin foil, bake at 350 degrees F for 10 minutes, then uncover the dish and cook the lasagna for 10 minutes more.

6. Cool the mixture down a bit, slice and serve.

Enjoy!

Lentils Lasagna

This is a superb dish! Try it and see!

Preparation Time: 10 minutes

Cooking Time: 50 minutes

Servings: 6

Ingredients:

- 14 ounces lasagna noodles, cooked
- 15 ounces canned red lentils, drained
- 2 tablespoons olive oil
- 1 yellow onion, chopped
- 1 pound carrots, peeled and chopped
- ½ pounds raw sunflower seeds mixed with 1 cup water and 1 tablespoon vegetable stock powder
- A pinch of salt and black pepper
- A pinch of nutmeg, ground
- 1 quart tomato juice
- 4 tablespoons vegan cream
- A pinch of marjoram, dried
- ½ tablespoon brown sugar

Method:

1. Heat up a pan with the oil over medium high heat, add the onion, stir and sauté for 2 minutes.

2. Add the carrots, sunflower seeds mix, salt, pepper and nutmeg, stir and cook for 5 more minutes.

3. Add the lentils, stir, simmer for 5-6 minutes more, transfer to a blender and pulse until you obtain a paste.

4. Put the tomato juice in a pot, add the vegan cream, marjoram, sugar, salt and pepper, bring to a simmer and cook over medium heat for 10 minutes.

5. Layer 3 lasagna noodles on the bottom of a baking dish, add 1/3 of the lentils mix, then spoon some of the tomato sauce.

6. Repeat with the rest of the ingredients, bake the lasagna at 400 degrees F for 40 minutes, cool it down a bit, slice and serve.

Enjoy!

Broccoli and Carrot Lasagna

Get ready to try something new and different!

Preparation Time: 10 minutes

Cooking Time: 40 minutes

Servings: 4

Ingredients:

- 4 cups steamed broccoli, chopped
- 2 cups steamed carrot, chopped
- 3 and ¾ cup cashew cheese, shredded
- 14 ounces lasagna noodles, cooked
- 20 ounces canned vegan cream of mushroom soup
- 1 teaspoon garlic powder
- 1 teaspoon rosemary, dried
- 2 teaspoons sweet paprika
- A pinch of salt and black pepper

Method:

1. In a bowl, mix cream of mushroom soup with 2 and ½ cups of the cashew cheese and stir well.

2. In another bowl, mix 1 and ¼ cups of this mushroom soup mix with broccoli, carrots, salt, pepper, garlic powder, paprika and rosemary and stir.

3. Layer 3 lasagna noodles on the bottom of a baking dish, spread ½ of the veggie mix, then layer 3 more lasagna noodles, then add a layer of cream of mushroom soup and half of the remaining cashew cheese.

4. Repeat the layers with the rest of the ingredients, top with cashew cheese, bake at 375 degrees F for 40 minutes, cool down, slice and serve.

Enjoy!

Celery Lasagna

It's one of the most delicious ones!

Preparation Time: 10 minutes

Cooking Time: 2 hours

Servings: 6

Ingredients:

- 1 cup dried porcini mushrooms, rehydrated
- 4 tablespoons butter
- ¼ cup olive oil
- 4 cups mushrooms, sliced
- A pinch of salt and black pepper
- 2 shallots, chopped
- 1 bay leaf
- 2 sage springs
- 2 rosemary springs
- 2 thyme springs
- 1 pound celery, chopped
- 3 leeks, chopped
- ½ cup marsala
- 4 cups veggie stock
- 2 and ½ cups coconut cream
- 4 cups cashew cheese, shredded
- 1 and ½ pounds lasagna noodles
- 1 cup basil, chopped

Method:

1. Heat up a pan with 2 tablespoons butter and half of the oil over medium heat, add all the mushrooms, salt and pepper, stir, cook for 10 minutes and transfer to a bowl.

2. Heat up the same pan with the rest of the butter and the rest of the oil over medium heat, add celery, bay leaf, rosemary, sage and thyme, stir and cook for 7 minutes.

3. Add the leeks, stir and cook for 6 minutes more.

4. Return the mushrooms to the pan, stir and cook for another 3 minutes.

5. Add the marsala, stir and cook for 5 minutes more.

6. Add half of the stock, half of the coconut cream, stir and cook for 10 minutes.

7. Heat up another pan with the rest of the cream and the rest of the stock, stir, bring to a simmer over medium heat and cook for about 10 minutes.

8. Take off the heat, add 1/3 of the cheese and whisk well.

9. Arrange a layer of lasagna noodles on the bottom of the baking dish, spread a layer of the mushrooms mix, then all a layer of the creamy sauce you've made, sprinkle some of the cheese and all the basil.

10. Repeat the action with the rest of the ingredients, top with the remaining cashew cheese, bake the lasagna at 360 degrees F for 1 hour, cool down a bit, slice and serve.

Enjoy!

Squash Lasagna

Gather all the ingredients and get started!

Preparation Time: 10 minutes

Cooking Time: 1 hour and 10 minutes

Servings: 6

Ingredients:

- 3 and ½ pounds butternut squash, peeled and cubed
- A pinch of salt and black pepper
- 4 tablespoons olive oil
- ½ cup coconut cream
- 1 pound cashew ricotta cheese
- 1 pound cashew cheese, shredded
- A pinch of nutmeg, ground
- 1 and ¼ cups veggie stock
- 1/3 cups sage, chopped
- 15 ounces lasagna noodles, cooked

Method:

1. Spread the squash on a lined baking sheet, and drizzle half of the oil, season with a pinch of salt and pepper, bake at 425 degrees F for 30 minutes and transfer to a bowl.

2. In a bowl, mix the cashew ricotta with the cream, half of the cashew cheese and nutmeg and stir well.

3. Heat up a pan with the rest of the oil over medium high heat, add the sage, cook it for 3 minutes and transfer to a bowl.

4. Add the squash, salt, pepper and the stock, mash everything a bit and then stir it well.

5. Spread ¾ cup of the ricotta mix on the bottom of a baking dish, and then add a layer of lasagna noodles, spread half of the squash mix and then top with a layer of lasagna noodles.

6. Spread 1 more cup of the ricotta mix and then repeat the layering with the remaining ingredients.

7. Sprinkle the rest of the cashew cheese all over, bake the lasagna at 375 degrees F for 35 minutes, cool it down, slice and serve.

Enjoy!

Squash and Spinach Lasagna

This is so yummy!

Preparation Time: 10 minutes

Cooking Time: 50 minutes

Servings: 6

Ingredients:

- 2 cups butternut squash puree
- ½ cup almond milk
- 1 cup cashew ricotta cheese
- A pinch of salt and white pepper
- ¼ teaspoon nutmeg, ground
- For the spinach mix:
- 8 ounces spinach, torn
- 1 cup cashew ricotta cheese
- 1 cup cashew cheese, shredded
- 2 garlic cloves, minced
- For the rest of the lasagna:
- 2 cups cashew cheese, shredded
- 10 ounces lasagna noodles, cooked
- ¼ teaspoon sweet paprika
- ¼ teaspoon basil, dried
- ¼ teaspoon Italian seasoning

Method:

1. In your food processor, mix the squash with the milk, 1 cup cashew ricotta, salt, pepper and nutmeg, pulse a bit and transfer to a bowl.

2. In another bowl, mix the spinach with 1 cup cashew ricotta, 1 cup cashew cheese and the garlic and stir well.

3. Spread 1/3 of the butternut squash in a baking dish, then sprinkle some of the 2 remaining cups of cashew cheese.

4. Add a layer of lasagna noodles, then spread half of the spinach mix and top with some of the cashew cheese again

5. Repeat the layers until you finish all the ingredients, sprinkle the rest of the cashew cheese, paprika, basil and Italian seasoning, cover the dish, bake the lasagna at 375 degrees F for 30 minutes, uncover and cook for 10 minutes more.

6. Cool the lasagna down, slice and serve.

Enjoy!

Squash and Caramelized Onion Lasagna

The caramelized onion gives this lasagna such an amazing taste!

Preparation Time: 10 minutes

Cooking Time: 1 hour and 40 minutes

Servings: 4

Ingredients:

- 6 cups butternut squash, peeled and cubed
- 2 tablespoons olive oil
- 2 tablespoons sage, chopped
- 12 garlic cloves, peeled
- Cooking spray
- A pinch of salt and black pepper
- 1 big onion, chopped
- 2 tablespoons water
- 18 ounces spinach, torn
- 1 bay leaf
- 5 cups coconut milk
- 5 tablespoons flour
- 1 thyme spring
- 1 and ½ cups cashew cheese, shredded
- ¼ teaspoon nutmeg, ground
- 12 ounces no-boil lasagna noodles

Method:

1. Spread the squash on a lined baking dish, spray cooking oil all over, add half of the olive oil as well, garlic, sage, salt and pepper, toss, bake at 425 degrees F for 30 minutes, transfer squash and garlic to a bowl and mash with a fork.

2. Heat up a pot with the rest of the oil over medium high heat, add the onion, toss and sauté for 5 minutes.

3. Reduce heat to low, cook the onion for 20 minutes more stirring often and transfer it to a bowl.

4. Heat up the pot again over medium heat, add the spinach and the water, toss, cook for 2 minutes, drain, transfer to the bowl with the onion and stir.

5. Heat up another pot with the milk over medium heat, add the bay leaf and the thyme, toss, bring to a boil, discard the thyme and bay leaf, add the flour, whisk, cook until it thickens, take off the heat, add half of the cashew cheese and the nutmeg and whisk well.

6. Spread ½ cup of this sauce on the bottom of a baking dish, layer 3 lasagna noodles, then add half of the squash mix, half of the caramelized onion and spinach mix and top with ¾ cup of the mil sauce.

7. Repeat the layers with the rest of the ingredients, sprinkle the rest of the cashew cheese on top, bake at 425 degrees F for 30 minutes, cool the lasagna down a bit, slice and serve.

Enjoy!

Leek Lasagna

You will make this again!

Preparation Time: 10 minutes

Cooking Time: 50 minutes

Servings: 6

Ingredients:

- 2 tablespoons olive oil
- 4 leeks, sliced
- 2 red onions, chopped
- ¼ pound spinach, torn
- ½ pound cashew ricotta
- 1 quart tomato sauce
- 14 ounces lasagna noodles, cooked
- 1 cup cashew cheese, shredded
- A pinch of salt and black pepper

Method:

1. Heat up a pan with the oil over medium high heat, add the leeks and the onions, toss and cook for 10 minutes.

2. Add the spinach, stir, cook for 3 minutes more and take off the heat.

3. In a bowl, mix the cashew ricotta with the leeks mixture, salt and pepper and stir well.

4. Spoon ¼ of the tomato sauce on the bottom of a baking dish, add a layer of lasagna sheers, spread half of the leeks mix and then top with 1/3 of the remaining tomato sauce.

5. Repeat the action with the rest of the ingredients, sprinkle the cashew cheese on top and bake the lasagna at 350 degrees F for 30 minutes.

6. Cool it down, slice and serve.

Enjoy!

Swiss Chard Lasagna

You have never tried something like this before!

Preparation Time: 10 minutes

Cooking Time: 1 hour

Servings: 8

Ingredients:

For the sauce:

- 1 bay leaf
- 2 and ½ cups almond milk
- 6 tablespoons coconut oil, melted
- ¼ cup flour
- A pinch of salt and white pepper
- ½ teaspoon nutmeg, ground
- A pinch of cloves, ground

For the Swiss chard mix:

- 1 pound Swiss chard, chopped
- 4 tablespoons olive oil
- 1 and 1/3 cups onion, chopped
- 4 garlic cloves, minced
- 1 pound cremimi mushrooms, chopped
- ¼ teaspoon nutmeg, ground

For the lasagna:

- 15 ounces lasagna noodles, cooked
- 15 ounces cashew ricotta cheese
- 12 ounces cashew cheese, shredded

Method:

1. Heat up a pot with the coconut oil over medium heat, add the bay leaf, the almond milk, flour, cloves, ½ teaspoon nutmeg, salt and pepper, whisk, cook for a few minutes until the sauce thickens and take off the heat.

2. Heat up a pan with half of the oil over medium high heat, add the onion, garlic and Swiss chard, stir, cook for 4 minutes and transfer to a bowl.

3. Heat up the same pan with the rest of the oil over medium heat, add the mushrooms, salt, pepper and ¼ teaspoon nutmeg, toss, cook for 8 minutes, transfer to the bowl with the Swiss chard and stir.

4. In a bowl, mix the cashew ricotta with half of the cashew cheese and stir.

5. Spoon some of the white sauce you've made on the bottom of a baking dish, layer 3 lasagna noodles over it, then spread half of the Swiss chard and mushroom mix and some of the cashew ricotta as well.

6. Continue the layers with the rest of the ingredients, top with the rest of the cashew cheese, cover the dish with tin foil, bake at 400 degrees F for 30 minutes, uncover, cook for 20 minutes more, cool down, slice and serve.

Enjoy!

Dessert Lasagna Recipes

We don't want you to skip dessert! Therefore, we searched and we discovered that you can make some pretty amazing dessert lasagnas! Here are the best and most delicious dessert lasagna recipes!

Peanut Butter Lasagna

It tastes so amazing and sweet!

Preparation Time: 1 day

Cooking Time: 0 minutes

Servings: 4

Ingredients:

- 14 ounces nutter butter cookies
- 1 cup cool whipped cream
- ½ cup peanut butter, melted
- 2 cups vanilla pudding, prepared

Method:

1. Arrange a layer of nutter butter cookies on the bottom of a baking dish.

2. Add a layer of peanut butter, then ½ of the pudding, half of the whipped cream and top with butter cookies.

3. Repeat the action with the rest of the ingredients, cool the lasagna down in the fridge for 1 day, slice and serve.

Enjoy!

Rich Chocolate Lasagna

If you love chocolate, you will love this lasagna as well!

Preparation Time: 30 minutes

Cooking Time: 0 minutes

Servings: 4

Ingredients:

- 36 regular Oreo cookies, crumbled
- ¼ cup sugar
- 8 ounces cream cheese, soft
- 6 tablespoon butter, melted
- 3 and ¼ cups cold milk
- 12 ounces cool whipped cream
- 7 ounces chocolate pudding mix
- ½ cup mini chocolate chips

Method:

1. In a bowl, mix the crumbled cookies with the butter stir, spread well on the bottom of a baking dish and keep in the fridge for 10 minutes.

2. In a bowl, mix the cream cheese with 2 tablespoons of cold milk, sugar and ¼ cups of whipped cream, beat well with a mixer, spread over the cookie layer and keep in the fridge for 10 minutes.

3. In a bowl, mix the rest of the milk with the pudding mix, stir well, spread over the cream cheese layer in the baking dish and keep in the fridge for 10 minutes more.

4. Spread the rest of the whipped cream on top of the lasagna, sprinkle the chocolate chips, cut the lasagna and serve.

Enjoy!

Strawberry Lasagna

It's a delicious and special sweet lasagna!

Preparation Time: 4 hours and 10 minutes

Cooking Time: 4 minutes

Servings: 8

Ingredients:

- 2 pounds strawberries, sliced
- 3 and ¾ cups heavy cream
- 1 teaspoon vanilla extract
- 1/3 cup powdered sugar
- ½ teaspoon rosewater
- 18 ounces graham crackers
- 2 ounces dark chocolate, chopped

Method:

1. In a bowl, mix 3 and ½ cups cream with sugar, vanilla and rosewater and stir using your mixer.

2. Spread a spoonful of this mix on the bottom of a baking dish, layer 6 graham crackers, then, add some more rosewater cream mix and then arrange a layer of strawberries.

3. Repeat the action again with the rest of the ingredients making sure you top with rosewater cream and strawberries and put the lasagna in the fridge for now.

4. Put the rest of the whipped cream in a small pot, add the chocolate, heat up over medium heat, stir well for 3-4 minutes and take off the heat.

5. Drizzle this over the strawberry lasagna and keep it in the fridge for 4 hours before serving.

Enjoy!

Milky Lasagna

Your kids will love this dessert lasagna!

Preparation Time: 6 hours and 10 minutes

Cooking Time: 0 minutes

Servings: 6

Ingredients:

- 8 ounces chips cookies
- 1 and ½ cups milk
- 14 ounces cool whipped cream
- Hot fudge sauce for serving

Method:

1. Arrange a layer of cookies on the bottom of a baking dish after you have dipped them into the milk.

2. Add a layer of whipped cream and then repeat the process with the rest of the ingredients.

3. Drizzle the hot fudge all over and keep the lasagna in the fridge for 6 hours before serving.

Enjoy!

Sweet Lasagna

Your guests will love this dessert!

Preparation Time: 1 hour and 10 minutes

Cooking Time: 8 minutes

Servings: 6

Ingredients:

- 12 ounces Oreo cookies, crumbled
- 2 tablespoons butter, melted
- 12 ounces cream cheese, soft
- 1 cup sugar
- 1 teaspoon lemon juice
- 8 ounces cool whipped cream
- 6 ounces chocolate pudding
- 3 cups milk
- 10 drops red food coloring
- For the top layer:
- 1 cup chocolate chips
- 8 ounces cool whipped cream

Method:

1. In a bowl, mix the Oreo cookies with the butter, stir, spread on the bottom of a baking dish and bake at 350 degrees F for 8 minutes.

2. In a bowl, mix 8 ounces cream cheese with sugar, lemon juice and 8 ounces whipped cream and blend using a mixer.

3. In another bowl, mix the milk with chocolate pudding, the rest of the cream cheese and food coloring and stir well.

4. Spread the cream cheese mix over the cookie crust, then spread the chocolate mix.

5. In a bowl, mix the chocolate chips 8 ounces whipped cream, stir well, spread over the sweet lasagna, keep it in the fridge for 1 hour, slice and serve.

Enjoy!

Minty Sweet Lasagna

This is perfect for a summer dessert!

Preparation Time: 15 minutes

Cooking Time: 0 minutes

Servings: 12

Ingredients:

- 16 ounces mint Oreo cookies
- 1 cup milk
- 16 ounces cool whipped cream
- ¼ teaspoon mint extract
- 8 ounces cream cheese
- ½ cup sugar
- 4 drops green extract
- 3 ounces chocolate pudding, prepared

Method:

1. Dip the cookies in the milk and arrange them on the bottom of a baking dish.

2. In a bowl, mix half of the whipped cream with mint extract, sugar, cream cheese and green extract, stir well and spread over the cookies.

3. Spread the pudding over the cream cheese mix and top with the rest of the whipped cream.

4. Keep the lasagna in the fridge for a while before serving.

Enjoy!

Pumpkin Lasagna

You have got to try this!

Preparation Time: 4 hours and 10 minutes

Cooking Time: 0 minutes

Servings: 6

Ingredients:

- 8 ounces cream cheese
- 1 and ½ cups heavy cream
- 2 cups milk
- ¼ cup sugar
- 3 small vanilla pudding packages
- 1 cup pumpkin puree
- 10 graham crackers
- 1 teaspoon pumpkin pie spice
- ¼ cup caramel, melted

Method:

1. In a bowl, mix the cream cheese with the sugar and the heavy cream and blend well using your mixer.

2. In another bowl, mix the vanilla pudding with the milk, pumpkin and pumpkin pie spice and blend really well.

3. Spread a layer of cream cheese mix on the bottom of a baking dish, then arrange a layer of graham crackers and half of the pumpkin mix.

4. Repeat the action once more with the remaining ingredients, drizzle the caramel at the end and keep the lasagna in the fridge for 4 hours before serving.

Enjoy!

Apple Lasagna

Here's an awesome autumn dessert!

Preparation Time: 1 hour

Cooking Time: 15 minutes

Servings: 8

Ingredients:

- 6 apples, peeled and chopped
- 2 tablespoons flour
- Juice of 1 lemon
- ½ cup brown sugar
- ½ teaspoon apple pie spice
- 2 teaspoons cinnamon powder
- 2 tablespoons maple syrup
- 8 ounces cream cheese
- 1 cup white sugar
- ½ cup heavy cream
- ½ teaspoon vanilla extract
- 2 tablespoons caramel, melted
- 16 ounces cool whipped cream
- 16 ounces graham crackers

Method:

1. Put the apples in a pan, heat up over medium heat, add lemon juice, flour, brown sugar, 1 teaspoon cinnamon, apple pie spice and maple syrup, stir, bring to a simmer, cook for 15 minutes and then cool down.

2. In a bowl, mix the cream cheese with the white sugar, 1 teaspoon cinnamon, heavy cream, vanilla extract, caramel and 8 ounces cool whipped cream and blend using your mixer.

3. Arrange a layer of crackers on the bottom of a baking dish, then spread half of the apples mix and also half of the cream cheese mix.

4. Repeat the action with the rest of the crackers, apples and cream cheese mixtures, spread 8 ounces whipped cream at the end and keep the lasagna in the fridge for 1 hour before serving.

Enjoy!

Delicious Mango Lasagna

Here's a unique and amazing dessert lasagna for you to try today!

Preparation Time: 2 hours and 10 minutes

Cooking Time: 6 minutes

Servings: 12

Ingredients:

- 8 ounces soft cream cheese
- ¾ cup coconut flakes
- 15 ounces cream of coconut
- 1 tablespoon rum
- 3 cups heavy cream
- 28 graham crackers
- 5 mangos, peeled and cubed
- 2 tablespoons sugar

Method:

1. Spread the coconut flakes on a lined baking sheet, toast at 350 degrees F for 6 minutes, and cool them down.

2. In a bowl, mix the cream cheese with the coconut cream and blend using your mixer.

3. Add the heavy cream, sugar and the rum and blend really well.

4. Spread some of the cream on the bottom of a baking dish, then arrange a layer of graham crackers, continue with another layer of cream and a layer of mango.

5. Repeat the action with the rest of the crackers, cream and end with a layer of mango.

6. Keep this in the fridge for 2 hours before serving.

Enjoy!

Ice Cream Lasagna

This is the perfect summer dessert idea!

Preparation Time: 1 hour and 10 minutes

Cooking Time: 0 minutes

Servings: 12

Ingredients:

- 24 ice cream sandwiches
- 12 ounces of fudge ice cream topping, melted
- 16 ounces peanut butter, soft
- 4 ounces chocolate pudding milk
- 16 ounces cool whipped cream
- 12 ounces of caramel ice cream topping, melted
- 16 peanut butter cups, chopped

Method:

1. Arrange 12 ice cream sandwiches on the bottom of a baking dish and spread half of the peanut butter over them.

2. In a bowl, mix the whipped cream with the chocolate pudding, whisk well and spread half of this mix over the peanut butter.

3. Arrange half of the butter cups over the chocolate layer and drizzle half of the fudge and caramel topping.

4. Repeat the layers with the rest of the ingredients and freeze the lasagna for 1 hour before serving.

Enjoy!

Conclusion

This has been such an amazing culinary experience! We've all discovered some of the best and most delicious lasagna recipes in the world.

As you now know, lasagna is such a versatile dish you can prepare on many different occasions

There are so many lasagna recipes out there that can help you make a great impression at a family gathering or also at a fancy and elegant dinner party.

All in all, lasagnas are really delicious and you can become a start in the kitchen if you choose to try the ones suggested by us today.

Enjoy the best lasagna recipes ever and have a lot of fun cooking them

About the Author

Born in New Germantown, Pennsylvania, Stephanie Sharp received a Masters degree from Penn State in English Literature. Driven by her passion to create culinary masterpieces, she applied and was accepted to The International Culinary School of the Art Institute where she excelled in French cuisine. She has married her cooking skills with an aptitude for business by opening her own small cooking school where she teaches students of all ages.

Stephanie's talents extend to being an author as well and she has written over 400 e-books on the art of cooking and baking that include her most popular recipes.

Sharp has been fortunate enough to raise a family near her hometown in Pennsylvania where she, her husband and children live in a beautiful rustic house on an extensive piece of land. Her other passion is taking care of the furry members of her family which include 3 cats, 2 dogs and a potbelly pig named Wilbur.

Watch for more amazing books by Stephanie Sharp coming out in the next few months.

Author's Afterthoughts

THANK you VERY MUCH!

I am truly grateful to you for taking the time to read my book. I cherish all of my readers! Thanks ever so much to each of my cherished readers for investing the time to read this book!

With so many options available to you, your choice to buy my book is an honour, so my heartfelt thanks at reading it from beginning to end!

I value your feedback, so please take a moment to submit an honest and open review on Amazon so I can get valuable insight into my readers' opinions and others can benefit from your experience.

Thank you for taking the time to review!

Stephanie Sharp

For announcements about new releases, please follow my author page on Amazon.com!

(Look for the Follow Bottom under the photo)

You can find that at:

https://www.amazon.com/author/stephanie-sharp

or Scan **QR-code** *below.*

Made in the USA
Monee, IL
16 February 2025